✓ B&T
$7.95

D0811837

Ethics and the Search for a Good Death

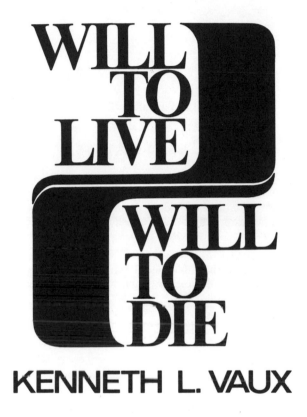

WILL
TO
LIVE
WILL
TO
DIE

KENNETH L. VAUX

Augsburg Publishing House
Minneapolis, Minnesota

Wingate College Library

WILL TO LIVE/WILL TO DIE

Copyright © 1978 Augsburg Publishing House

Library of Congress Catalog Card No. 78-52188

International Standard Book No. 0-8066-1659-8

All rights reserved. No part of this book may be used or reproduced in any manner whatsoever without written permission except in the case of brief quotations embodied in critical articles and reviews. For information address Augsburg Publishing House, 426 South Fifth Street, Minneapolis, Minnesota 55415.

Scripture quotations unless otherwise noted are from the Revised Standard Version of the Bible, copyright 1946, 1952, and 1971 by the Division of Christian Education of the National Council of Churches.

MANUFACTURED IN THE UNITED STATES OF AMERICA

Contents

076181

Acknowledgments

In the past several years our ongoing programs in medical humanities at the Institute of Religion and Baylor College of Medicine have been enriched by a new circle of colleagues that has joined the University of Texas units in the Houston Center. I would like to acknowledge the insight and inspiration received from Drs. Bill Bartholome, Margery Shaw, Don Hayes, Henry Strobel, Rod Howell and Charles Scott. To my colleagues at the M. D. Anderson Hospital: Drs. Jan vanEys, Emil Freireich, Margaret Sullivan, Watura Sutow, Ayten Cangir, Richard Lucas and Steven Culbert, I owe the clinical insights that characterize this book .

Finally, to a young woman whom I first met at Anderson whose final task was to train many of us in what this depth of life is all about—Laurie—your smile and strength have been an inspiration to us all. I dedicate this to you.

KENNETH VAUX

Introduction

The Task

IN 1971 A FILM APPEARED at theaters around the world that has developed a more passionate cult following than any film of the decade. *Harold and Maude* is the story of a redoubtable old lady (near 80) whose lust for living keeps her young and endears her to young Harold (near 20), whose obsessive interest in death leads him to try a variety of methods, all hilarious, to do himself in. The story ends with a bizarre but somehow natural transmutation as Maude, prompted by love of life, takes the suicide pill on her eightieth birthday. At the same time, a redeeming, caring sorrow for his lost friend transforms Harold's morbid compulsions into a will to live on.

This is a book about human initiatives in death. It asks whether there is a different kind of suicide, a new form of willful death, precipitated by the life-world we have fashioned by our technology. It asks whether there is a new kind of *intended death* that may be fitting, perhaps even morally licit.

The impulse to kill, the wish to die, have always been viewed as aberrations, as departures from our sense of who we are and what we are meant to be. Such an impulse or wish distorts the primal biological instincts of survival. It violates the basic moral structures of reality, because homicide and suicide do violence to life seen as trust. The common law has sought to embody this natural and moral insight by proscribing suicide as a species of homicide. In our tradition, therefore, "intending death" for oneself or another is a sickness, a sin and a crime.

The qualitatively new issue is generated by our technical prowess. It is now increasingly possible to prevent and intervene death. This development mandates human deliberation and decision at the conclusion of life. In previous generations death would steal in with frightful, unexpected suddenness or grind on with inexorable fatality. While much of the world still knows death as a "thief in the night," or the cruel inevitability of the way things are, the traditional before-death posture of watching and waiting is slowly yielding a new response: *prepare and decide*.

In America today there exists a large subculture of people who are waiting around to die. They populate the nursing homes, retirement communities and medical center hotels of this world. A large circle of people with fatal diagnoses, waiting and preparing to die, is a new phenomenon in human history. Because of the moral ambivalence in our culture toward death, we commit this community of persons to a frightful limbo. These persons wait for death in a culture committed to life preservation. The malice of this suspended animation is caused by that ambivalence which says simultaneously: "You must live" and "We have no need of you." If we choose to extend the life span, we could at least honor our elders as the Azerbaijan mountain people on the steppes of Asia do. Here octogenarians are indispensable to the future of society. At eighty they are just coming into their own as workers and sages. How cruel to preserve life, yet not render it vibrant and vital.

In addition to those deaths awaited with anticipation at the end of a full life, there is another mode of intended death brought into being by advancing technology. Here an injury or illness inflicts psychic, emotional, and interrelational mortality, but medical ingenuity intervenes the physical death. The Zygmaniak case [1] is an example of this. Here a young man was driving his motorcycle on a treacherous path, hit an obstruction and was thrown to the ground, snapping his neck and sustaining a high spinal cord injury. He was taken to surgery to see if restoration were possible. When it was not, he asked his brother to shoot him. The strong, rugged young man chose not to live the rest of his life as a quadriplegic. Technology had the power to keep his head alive and prohibit general deterioration in the rest of his body. He chose not to live like that.

Similarly, persons on dialysis have chosen to neglect their diets, allow the machine to get dirty and through disregard of a life-prolonging mechanism indirectly hasten their deaths. Two young women in my clinical experience have tired of the rigors of regular dialysis, the burdens of struggling for some imperfect measure of life at great cost and family strain, and have chosen to hasten death.

Such cases may become more typical. As biomedical technology presents us with more devices to replace or empower the failing functions of our bodies, we will find the survival instinct and will-to-live energy thrown more and more into conflict with what might be called the "will to give in." Emotional, volitional and moral tensions of a magnitude heretofore unknown in human experience will be activated.

But even if our culture can rekindle the grace of honoring the aged and accepting death intention in the very sick, we must also face the new challenge of choosing death under certain circumstances.

Socrates could have escaped. Jesus could have eased Pilate out of his bind. Yet Socrates would not accept Crito's advice to leave town, and Jesus set his face steadfastly towards Jerusalem. But we are neither martyrs nor saints. Yet we are being forced into making judgments regarding the time and manner of our death. Courage becomes the necessity of our freedom. Although suicide and martyrdom are infrequent, the freedom of choice once reserved for philosophers, prophets, and soldiers is becoming commonplace. "Laying down one's life"—the noble fate of great persons down through the ages—now becomes the difficult choice that almost all of us must face. Stripped of the innocence of fate and the glory of self-sacrifice, we are more and more going to be required to make "elective death" our last decision, that is, we will have the power to choose the moment and manner of our death.

Choosing death is one characteristic of our last quest for responsibility.[2] Comforting mythologies have lost their grip. The rationalizations that sustained our parents against the enigma of death come harder to us. To be the first generation entrusted with power over the dying process is like the enhanced duty at the inception of life. In birth and death we must awkwardly struggle to live responsibly with the new awareness of who we are and what we can do. Deliberating and choosing a human death is a new dimension of our freedom.

This book seeks to guide us along the process of reflection, personal decision, and public policy formulation that is now required. We are reluctant to come to terms with the facts about human initiatives in death. There is little doubt that we unconsciously intend death for ourselves by the reckless ways we live. Through neglect and hostility we slowly kill one another, at least in the New Testament sense of that term. "Every one who is angry with his brother . . . who insults his brother shall be liable to judgment" (Matthew 5:21-22).

We know that people have taken their own lives or the lives of others in great numbers down through the ages. Most often these intended deaths have been camouflaged to look like accidents. One author [3] poses the provocative thesis that the extraordinary growth in population beginning in the nineteenth century is not attributable to science, or even sanitation, but rather to the decline of infanticide. Parents stopped exposing, drowning and smothering their own children.

Whatever interpretations we make of our history, it is clear that new requirements of responsibility are upon us. Edwin

Schneidman puts it succinctly with reference to the manner of recording and certifying death:

> [the death certificate] should abandon the anachronistic Cartesian view of man as a passive biological vessel on which the fates work their will, and instead reflect the contemporary view of man as a psycho-socio-biological organism that can, and in many cases does, play a significant role in hastening its own demise. This means that the death certificate should contain at least one item on the decedent's intention vis-a-vis his own death.[4]

The literature on death and dying is proliferate, if not promiscuous. Courses are taught in colleges and high schools. The discussion of death and dying has become the fad and the fetish of our time.

Ours is an age of fascination with mortality, mingled with denial and repression. Analyses and interpretations are manifold. As in the eighteenth century, "pre" and "post" death literature abounds, along with letters and messages from the departed. Yet in the daily traffic of life the topic of death finds us awkward and embarrassed.

The paradoxical quality of our response to death, I will contend, gives a clue to its profound meaning. Ever since Geoffrey Gorer's essay on "The Pornography of Death"[5] in 1965 we have been aware of the mingled repression and fascination that characterize the Western perception of death. Malcolm Muggeridge notes that death has replaced sex as the forbidden subject: ". . . for most contemporary minds the notion of death is hidden away, unmentioned if not unmentionable, as the Victorians hid away the notion of sex."[6] In the 1970s, in our anti-Victorian culture, death has become an avantgarde topic of conversation, the subject of endless banter. Yet there remains the paradox of denial comingled with fascination. Richard Kalish makes the point:

> Death is blasphemous and pornographic. We react to it and its symbols in the same way as we react to any pornography. We avoid it. We deny it exists. We avert our eyes from its presence.

Wingate College Library

We protect little children from observing it and dodge their questions about it. We speak of it only in whispers. We consider it horrible, ugly and grotesque.[7]

Yet we must add that, as with pornographic material, we find death seductive; it lures us. We wish to sneak a peek.

This book seeks to interpret the paradox. I believe that death is an experience that incites contradictions in the human mind. A root paradox is activated in our sense of justice: the contradiction between what is and what ought to be. The responsible way to interpret death, therefore, is in terms of this paradox or tension. Death is both natural *and* unnatural, good *and* evil, desirable *and* undesirable, friend *and* enemy. This is the paradox, the tension, the mystery of death. We misunderstand death if we try to resolve this paradox. We endanger ourselves if we try to unscrew the inscrutable or make simple the mysterious.

The architecture of our thesis is a framework of tensions which set in motion a dialectic. After an initial chapter charting the dialectic, we will consider Intentional Death from the perspective of modern medicine (II), social culture (III) and our religious-moral world view (IV, V, VI), seeing that explanation and evaluation come into focus through use of this *paradox* lens. From this basic understanding we can then draw practical applications for public philosophy as well as for personal and collective ministries to the dying (VII).

The
Dialectical
Character of Death

I

HUMAN RESPONSE TO DEATH has always been full of contradictions. In contrast to the animals and plants, people reflect on death, anticipate it, fear it, and invest it with a variety of meanings. Like sheep led to the slaughter, the brute meets death with neither premonition or anticipation. Instinctual terror and flight (the hunted deer) and purposive self-sacrifice (the marching fire ants) are crude anticipations in nature of that root tension between living and dying that will become the paradoxical genius of man.

In a poignant response to the loss of his wife, Joy, to cancer, C. S. Lewis reflects on the painful, unique wonder that God has wrought in us:

> Sometimes Lord, one is tempted to say that if you wanted us to behave like the lilies of the field you might have given us an organization more like theirs. But that, I suppose, is just your grand experiment. Or no; not an experiment, for you have no need to find things out. Rather your grand enterprise. To make an organism which is also a spirit; to make that terrible oxymoron, a "spiritual animal." To take a poor primate, a beast with nerve-endings all over it, a creature with a stomach that wants to be filled, a breeding animal that wants to mate, and say, "now get on with it. Become a god!" [8]

Hegel's great interpreter, Koyéve, shows how the philosopher explicates this new quality of death that appears in man. Quoting Hegel: "The animal dies. But the death of the animal is the becoming of human consciousness." For man this tension becomes the environment for his creativity. "Man is the mortal sickness of nature. Man is not only mortal, he is death incarnate; he is his own death." For man death is not natural but violent. It is conscious of itself and voluntary. "Man's death and consequently true human existence are, in a manner of speaking, a suicide." [9]

In one sense all nature shares in the paradoxical energies of vitality and decay, affirmation and negation, life and death that heightens in man. The will to live and the willingness to die abide in tension in every living organism.

Eros and thanatos, biophilia and necrophilia—influence human experience. To follow the Freudian picture, there is openness to life, to the new, to the future. There is also the desire for closure, going back, nostalgia, retention, stillness. René Dubos reminds us that the tropical birds, particularly the male of the species, present this dual intentionality: the males are brightly colored, cocky, and strutting; while the drab female blends into the background. The beauty of the male insures ongoing life and death. It attracts the mate for procreation; it also attracts the predator. So it is in man. A highly developed cortex and nervous system makes both ecstasy and suffering possible. Senescence and senility, while seen to be natural, are often unwelcome developments. Aging seems to be written into the genetic code which is also the secret of growth. Cancer can be seen as hyperlife—life gone wild. The treatments must be anti-life. One of cancer's most dramatic agents—methotrexate— is an anti-vitamin. In man, life and death intermingle. Conception is a kind of death, both of sperm and ova. Like the grain of wheat that must fall to the ground and die before it can bring forth fruit, so in man death is the overture of birth. Dying, we are told, even in the clinical perspective, is a kind of birth.[10]

As the human mind pauses to reflect on the enigma of death, the same biting paradox is felt. In art and poetry, in architecture and philosophy, and in songs and stories, man tries to make sense of this mystery. The paradox is found in the earliest reflection of Western man. In the Greeks some thinkers accent flux, change, and death (Heraclitus, the Stoics), while others accent the changeless and immutable (Parmenides, Plato).

Roman wisdom kept the tension alive. For Seneca, death, while dreadful and final, was to be accepted with equanimity because of its reality and its purposiveness. Death reflects the tragic necessity of all matter. Yet the philosopher must both fear and desire death because of the "eagerness of the soul to return whence it came." Seneca used the phrase *libido moriendi* to describe a death attraction that offsets the death aversion.

In a similar manner the religious tradition locates this dual force in all of nature.[11] In the *Gilgamesh Epic*, Siduri says to Gilgamesh: "When the gods created humanity they established death for mankind; they kept life in their own hands" (Tablet X, iii, 3-4). The root myths in all religions suggest that human death signals a rupture in the creation; something has gone wrong. Man's immortal nature has been sullied or changed by his grasp for natural immortality. He has aroused the anger of the gods. While man has life (breath) he is always aware of the tenuousness of this vitality. The vital force is diminished by sickness; it is always being drawn back to stillness. Just as the wind of God sweeps across the primal waters of creation, so the breath of God sustains life in man for a short time. Like the life-giving energy, the exhausting power of the Creator Spirit always hovers near. Whenever the human spirit ponders death it frames these reflections in a paradoxical mode.[12]

As personal beings we receive our mortality in a similarly dialectical way. The clinical study of dying, pioneered by Beatrix Cobb at M. D. Anderson Hospital in Houston, was conveyed by Institute of Religion Chaplains Carl Neiswonger and Herman Cook to Elisabeth Kübler-Ross at Billings Hospital in Chicago. This work has shown the dialectics of resistance and readiness,

disbelief and embrace, anger and acceptance that describe the way people meet death in hospitals. This is all the more amazing since death so often occurs today in the centers of medicine which are given to healing, life affirmation, and prolongation of vitality. Even here the alternate energies of resignation are invariably expressed, even though the atmosphere encourages hope and denial.

The lively debate between life and death in our being is the portrayal of that existential search for what life is all about. That tension between self-affirmation and self-sacrifice—that search which the New Testament calls losing oneself in order to find oneself (Matthew 10:39)—is the road map of the human pilgrimage. Ernest Becker,[13] who died of cancer in 1974, was passionately caught up in this dialog. In a letter to a friend he wrote:

> . . . Life seeks to secure itself, and it also seeks the furtherance of other life, Therefore the feeling of failure and futile death is rooted in our very being. . . . Somehow one has to let go, without dying. One has to come to (the) brink of destruction, and then relax and accept his life. . . . Suicide is a way out, but it ends the dialogue.[14]

In the arena of public philosophy we grope along toward a social policy on death that is humane and acceptable. Two million people have registered living wills to indicate their acceptance of death and their fear that impersonal forces might cause their lives to be needlessly prolonged. Many states have adopted Natural Death statutes and most others now have such bills in process. These laws release physicians and institutions from litigation when they honor their patients' intentions to not have their lives prolonged. Ambivalence at a societal level mirrors that basic paradox we find in human reflection and experience. Weisman and Hackett have summarized: "It is our paradoxical attitude toward death, not the fact of death itself, that makes insoluble conflicts seem inevitable." [15]

One might conclude from this discussion that a problem

that must remain unresolved cannot be explored. But we should not hesitate to explore the questions and attempt new levels of insight and commitment that more faithfully reflect the paradox and mystery of death. More particularly, this book seeks to probe the moral question of appropriate initiatives in death in the light of our finest ethical wisdom and with candor regarding the kind of world we live in. We now turn to a description of the cultural phenomenon of intending death. Only on the basis of accurate knowledge of where our culture has come from can we hope to discuss intelligently where we ought to be.

II

Death in Modern Medicine

Dierdre

SHE WAS TWENTY-NINE YEARS OLD and a rare human being—spicy, unpredictable, comic. A funeral was not her wish She would have preferred a Chicago circus. She fought her leukemia like a tiger for three and a half years. Finally she submitted to a last-ditch protocol—a bone marrow transplant with powerful methotrexate chemotherapy following. The medication killed the graft. She conceded the operation much like she would have the autopsy—for the sake of the doctors and medical knowledge.

She was deeply devoted to her fellowmen: able to listen, to share, to elicit the things of beauty from each one. She was deeply spiritual in a non-religious way. She knew Elisabeth Kübler-Ross, whose monumental work on the stages of dying was begun by Beatrix Cobb years before at the Anderson. Life-after-death. Who knows? Maybe!

She fought death but not with desperation. She exuded a strong skeptical peace in all her dealings. A social work graduate student at the University of Texas, she was not preparing for a career—she *was* a career. She hoped she would survive.

21

She was ready not to. She possessed that uncanny composure known only to those who carry their death in their body.

She could die in peace—even under the full alarm rescue-resuscitation that rolled in as she lay dying. And that was all right. At her memorial we read the words of John Donne and Emily Dickinson:

> Death be not proud though some have called thee
> Mighty and dreadful, for thou art not so; . . .
> One short sleep past, we wake eternally,
> And Death shall be no more: Death, thou shalt die.[16]

> Though the great waters sleep,
> That they are still the deep,
> We cannot doubt—
> No vascillating God
> Ignited this abode
> To put it out— [17]

Our experience of what death is like and what it means is colored by the modern clinical setting: the hospital, and the developing science of biological medicine which slowly but irrevocably alters the way we think about dying. In this chapter we will look at what is happening in modern medicine and the setting where it is practiced. We will see that tensions or polarities characterize both the scientific advances and the hospital practices where this knowledge is applied to sick persons. The purpose of the chapter is to show how enlarged clinical sophistication to prolong life demands increased human responsibility in the arena of determinations of death.

The Present Clinical Situation

The following guidelines have just been issued to the clinical services in internal medicine at our medical college. An ad hoc committee of the Department of Medicine was asked to make policy recommendations for use in the clinics in our teaching hospitals.

Here is their report:

A person will be considered dead if in the announced opinion of a physician, based on ordinary standards of medical practice he has experienced as irreversible cessation of *spontaneous* respiratory and circulatory functions.

In the event that artificial means of support preclude a determination that these functions have ceased, a person will be considered dead if in the announced opinion of a physician, based upon ordinary standards of medical practice he has experienced as irreversible cessation of spontaneous brain functions. Death will have occurred at the time (when it is determined) the relevant functions ceased.[18]

The ordinary standards of medical practice for the determination of irreversible cessation of spontaneous brain function will be defined as follows:

A. *Clinical Criteria*

    1. The patient is comatose: there is no spontaneous movement.* No response can be elicited to painful stimuli, e.g. compression of the achilles tendon or of the testes.

    2. There is no spontaneous respiratory effort in that respiration must be maintained by artificial means.

    3. The following cephalic reflexes must be absent: pupillary, corneal, audio-ocular and oculocephalic.**

    4. The pupils are dilated (>5.0 mm).***

When these conditions have been present for *six* hours an electroencephalogram shall be recorded.

B. *EEG Criteria†*

    1. The EEG should show no evidence of electrical activity of brain origin for a period of not less than 30 minutes of continuous recording at a time when the clinical criteria shall have persisted unchanged for six hours.

    2. A second EEG made no less than six hours after the first should also demonstrate "electrocerebral silence."

C. *Special Procedure*

    In any situation in which there is a possible drug effect involved in the patient's altered state of consciousness, in situations in which there is doubt as to the nature of the pathological process, or in the situation where preservation of sound organs for transplantation requires that there not be any unnecessary delay in the determination of brain death, the condition of brain death may be established by cerebral perfusion studies which demonstrate cessation of intracranial circulation.[19]

Notes

*   "Spontaneous movement" does not include tremor or clonus of the lower extremities which may be present transiently as a consequence of hyperexcitability of spinal cord neurons resulting from release of descending cortical inhibitory influences.

**   The presence or absence of spinal or vestibular reflexes have been shown to have little relevance to survival.

***   A pupillary diameter of less than 5.0 mm increases the possibility that drug intoxication in involved. At this level of coma the EEG is of no value in determining if drug action is involved.

When the pupil is smaller than 5.0 mm, even if all other criteria are met, *serum drug level determinations* and/or *studies of cerebral blood flow* may be required to rule out the possibility of drug intoxication.

(Unless the nature of the underlying cause of the coma is clearly evident the possibility of drug intoxication is otherwise difficult to exclude.)

†   The EEG determination of electrocerebral silence shall be carried out according to the guidelines set forth by the American Electroencephalographic Society.

Since there is evidence to suggest that young children may survive longer periods of electrocerebral silence than adults, these criteria may not be applicable to children of less than about 5 years of age.[20]

Commentary

These guidelines attempt to maintain a delicate tension between objective criteria and subjective judgment in the determination of when a person is dead. To avoid the arbitrary and excessive in subjective medical judgment the physiologic and neural-electrical criteria are used. The radically antinomian position contends that a person is dead when a doctor declares him dead. Sometimes this orientation has led to death determinations that were premature in the light of objective criteria, e.g., the early transplant surgeons who desired to retrieve "fresh tissue" for donation. At other times subjective judgment has erred by artificially maintaining subhuman vitality when death has already set in, e.g., the case of keeping Generalissimo Franco on life supports until the political transition was secured.

On the other hand, dangers are recognized in the sole use of objective criteria to determine death. The wide range of physical and psychic variables, the ever wider range of expressions of vitality with or without medical assistance, render the clinical situation of dying and death one of infinite variability, where each case is unique. Objective guidelines can be instructive; but spontaneous, particularized judgments are always required.

The subtle nuances of these guidelines try to forestall attempts to initiate death in patients by passive or active euthanasia on the one hand by establishing baseline criteria which must be present before a decision to terminate treatment can be ethically made. On the other hand, there is the motive to legally and morally sanction efforts to suspend life-support intervention when there is no hope of recovery. In other words, clinicians want the best of both worlds. They want to be released from the burden of having to make moral discriminations by having objective, codified guidelines. But they also want to retain the freedom and autonomy to render private judgment. This is a futile quest. You can't have both. While it is true that medical science will make possible more accurate prognoses, more precise interpretations of physiologic trauma, more conclusive insights into what will happen to a person with this or that problem, it is also true that technology enables greater powers of resuscitation, vital function monitoring and manipulation along with greater capacity to delay inevitable morbid processes. There is no way to avoid the responsibility of qualitiative clinical judgment. Today's doctors must be as skilled in this as they are in quantitative analysis.

What can clinical medicine do to forestall or foreshorten the dying process? Five areas of therapeutics must be mentioned:

(1) Mechanical life supports. The mechanical respirator is the symbolic representative of a range of devices which assist or replace faltering or collapsed functions of the body. The heart-lung machine, ventricular assist (ALVAD), pacemaker, dialysis unit, computers and other electrical devices to effect neural regulation, the new mechanisms to dispense medicine into the systems (e.g. glaucoma and leukemia automated medicators) are other examples. Cardiac defibrillators, resuscitation devices and other external instruments must also be added to this armamentarium. The purpose of such instruments is to help an injured person through a traumatic crisis until normal function can be restored. Often the effect is to compensate permanently for a lost power. Some say that the sophisticated powers, used uncritically, now make possible the horrid parody of life where vegetative functions are sustained long after meaningful mental life is gone. It is now possible to support a brain mechanically even when the underlying physical organism has broken down. Karen Quinlan cases remind us of the moral ambivalence of these techniques.

(2) Regulation of blood components. The Hebrews knew what clinical medicine has discovered, that "life is in the blood." The river of life can be monitored and modified in myriad ways to regulate vitality. Nutrients can be directly infused. The new procedures of hyperalimentation are added to the former skills of keeping sugar, salt, trace metal and nutrient elements in balance. Electrolyte balance can be regulated. Blood components—platelets, plasma, red and white cells—can be added. Not only blood building but volume and pressure regulation and blood cleansing are possible through numerous techniques.

(3) Temperature monitoring and the regulation of metabolism are possible. Hypothermia is used in surgery to cool down the patient. Cryogenics holds forth the promise of longer range "anabiosis" for therapeutic effect or slowing down a disease process. Hyperthermia is now being used in some cancer patients to

heat up bodily processes in the hope of bolstering defensive capability, fighting alien process and promoting healing.

(4) Sedation is another area of therapeutic competence that makes the crisis of sickness amenable to human control. Pain can be alleviated in a variety of ways. Large doses of morphine can hasten death. Administration of oxygen can affect the body's own narcoticizing effect. Brompton's Mixture can ease the intractable pain of cancer. Marijuana and LSD and other hallucinogens may provide relief from some diseases.

(5) Finally, clinical medicine, through its sensitivity or insensitivity, can affect one's hope and will to live. How hospitals handle issues like honesty, conversation, simple courtesy and kindness—often so tragically abused in modern hospitals—probably affects the person's attitude toward death or life every bit as much as these therapeutic powers.

Recognizing many available life prolonging techniques, and acknowledging the moral absurdity of always doing whatever can be done, a committee of the Harvard Medical School and Massachusetts General Hospital has recently adopted guidelines for the "Optimum Care For Hopelessly Ill Patients." [21] Given the awesome powers of the new therapeutics, the guidelines commendably attempt to come to grips with the new burdens of responsibility in the clinical management of patients.

The guidelines state that, whenever appropriate, critically ill patients will be classified into four groups:

CLASS A: maximal therapeutic effort without reservation

CLASS B: maximal therapeutic effort without reservation but with daily evaluation because probability of survival questionable

CLASS C: selective limitation of therapeutic measures

CLASS D: all therapy can be discontinued

This individualized approach stresses the basic ethical safeguards, the physician's clinical judgment and the fully informed consent of the patient and/or the family. It goes beyond the traditional subjective criteria and the more recent impersonal tendency and wades into the troubled waters of real clinical situations. Certifying a person's death is not nearly as difficult as inclining the patient toward or away from death through treatment choices. The real day-to-day world of clinical therapeutics is filled with these life-changing decisions. The formidable challenge is that of maximizing the realm of human freedom so that decisions can be informed and self chosen.

First, this goal requires a disposition of *kindness* and care wherein the patient's best interests become those of the physician and the others who attend him. Putting oneself in the place of the patient is still the best method I know to provoke empathy, sympathy, and genuine respect of the other person. This has been called the Golden Rule in medicine.

An unfortunate kind of paternalism exists in medicine in which the doctor says, "It is best that I take over decisions for this person and spare her the anguish of having to think and decide for herself among alternate courses." This mentality is based on the sometimes mistaken notion that there is a preferred course of treatment for every disease at every stage. Working from this assumption, the doctor feels that it is best to go ahead and do what is indicated with as little deliberation and decision as possible on the patient's part.

Second, if kindness has become the primary disposition—subordinating busyness, efficiency, regulations, contempt and other malignant impulses—then *knowledge* is the next quality needed. A correct diagnosis of one's condition is absolutely necessary if there is to be any informed consent to treatment. Here we come face to face with a major heresy of the modern mind. Many people assume, on the basis of some facile psychology, that fear, guilt, stress, anxiety, and dread are diseased emotions which are best done away with by deception, drugs, "counseling" or any other behavior modification. As a result, we have come to depreciate our ability to deal with danger and the tragic reality of life. Feifel's studies on physicians' attitudes toward death [22] have shown a reluctance to "tell it like it is." Whereas most patients want to know their condition, most doctors hesitate to disclose fully the gravity of terminal conditions. Even Elisabeth Kübler-Ross, whose openness and accessibility to the dying patient has pioneered a new quality of care for the terminally ill, advises never to tell the patient he or she is dying.[23] Only when asked should the doctor venture into this forbidden realm of discourse.

This drives us back to the former point. In the modern myth of perfection, anxiety in the face of death is seen as neurosis, as disease to be obliterated from human consciousness. We need to recover the ancient theological sense that death awareness is a natural mechanism serving us as a truth messenger. Awareness of impending death calls us to authentic being, to reality, to truth. Disease itself, as a prefiguration of death, can be seen as a message, a voice, a beacon.[24] Because in our "natural end, there lie the most varied opportunities for the genesis of neurotic symptoms,"[25] compassionate, confronting honesty should be the attitude of physician to patient.

A third quality to be nurtured is *endurance*. The debilitating fear of abandonment must be allayed in patients so that not only kindness and knowledge, but also courageous endurance are elicited. The tension between the heroic and the accepting impulses in the physician correspond to the will to live/willingness to die tension that exists in the patient. It also corresponds to the families' wish to hold on or hope for a speedy end. The clinical environment, in other words, is a milieu where oscillations —sometimes frenzied, sometimes patterned—occur. Where concern, and not expediency, is uppermost, the hospital experience is characterized by the vital balance between optimism and realism.

A page from my personal diary illustrates this tension between the will to live and the willingness to die:

> Drs. Bill Trannum and Bob Cockburn led our entourage into the rooms of a dozen patients. In only three we found that vital tension inclined towards hope and possible recovery. In most of the cases the prognosis was discouraging. A twenty-two-year-

old man—four years into acute leukemia, now completely re-
fracted against treatment, nothing more to be done—only comfort and sedate. Another old man with acute renal failure and
progressive myeloma, etc., etc. In most of the cases treatment
was a holding operation. Recovery or remission was out of the
question. The goals were management, maximizing functional
capacity within the constraints imposed by the disease. The
moral dilemma is what I've seen so often. How shall the patient be accompanied toward death—transfusions? More cut
downs to find those elusive veins? Another round of chemotherapy? Antibiotics against this infection? Hyperalimentation?
Resuscitation?
An unspoken hope is felt beneath the surface. It is a hope that
the final crisis will come soon, that it will be sudden, that death
will steal in while we're not looking. A certain sadness is felt
at having to use various treatments which have only the salu-
tary effect of prolonging the dying process. But the patients,
for the most part, do not openly acknowledge that they are
dying. It is not mentioned, even if it is silently acknowledged.
Because of this denial, discussion of initiatives toward death is
impossible. Even deliberate weighing of alternatives and decisive choice of one or another approach is precluded. We stumble on, waiting for certain death—aware of the lethal time-
bomb awaiting the welcome visitor, unable to usher him in—
forced into gestures forestalling his visit.

This account reflects the experience of rounds in a typical
teaching hospital in a medium sized town on an adult cancer
service. The reflection would be different on a pediatric oncology
service. It would be different in a burn unit, an intensive coronary care unit, a diabetes clinic at a V.A. hospital. But though
the dialectics modulate differently in different settings, the
parameters of the human drama are the same.

The clinical environment of modern medicine is also influenced by the sometimes conflicting values of research and care.
In life-threatening illness, experimental treatments are often introduced which intensify the life-saving/death-accepting dialectic. The following reflection is based on my clinical work as
a consultant in ethics to the Pediatrics Department of the M. D.
Anderson Hospital and Cancer Research Center.

Meditation: *Lazarus Revisited*

When we are well and whole we forget that life is a story. It appears to be static, constant, eternal. It seems to consist of recurrent patterns, developmental sequences, cycles, coming and going, then coming again. Up at 6:30, to school at 7:30, home, dinner at 6, bed-snack, to sleep at 8:30. Yesterday and tomorrow—forever the same. Upward and downward trajectories, recurrent rhythms, stages of childhood, stages of decline, pre- and post-death stages—all the same, consistent, universal.

Sickness transforms life into a pilgrimage. Life is a drama, not the Greek analogy but the Semitic story; not recapitulating themes but once and for all, forever unique, unrepeatable persons on an adventure. Life is an epic of judgment and grace. It is understandable only within the dimension of spirit.

The patient is a pilgrim; the physician, a defender-companion. The unknown must be explored. One must go to meet the dark night. One strains to see dawn break as darkness somehow softens.

John Donne was 50 years old in 1621 when King James appointed him Dean of St. Paul's Cathedral. Shortly after he became seriously sick and developed pneumonia. After several days of precipitous danger both from the disease and the treatments, his health gradually returned. Donne imposed on this experience the leitmotivs of his thought: (1) estrangement and lethal sickness, (2) the Messiah as healer, without whom the physician is impotent, and (3) the raising of Lazarus. His *Devotions* chronicle the spiritual pilgrimage of fear and reckoning, abandonment and rescue, exhaustion and ecstasy that characterize life-threatening illness. The outline of the *Devotions* shows the signposts of those traveling pilgrims—patient and physician.

The First Grudging of the Sickness
The Patient Takes His Bed
The Physician Comes
The Physician Is Afraid
The Disease Steals on Insensibly

They Use Cordials to Keep the Disease from the Heart
They Apply Pigeons to Draw the Vapours from the Head
The Sickness Declares Its Malignity By Spots
I Sleep Not Day or Night
The Bell Tolls for Another Telling Me I Must Die
At Last the Physician Sees Land
God Prospers Their Practice and By Them He Calls Me,
    Lazarus, Out of My Bed [26]

Dr. William Easson has coined a new phrase for this medical literature, "The Lazarus Syndrome." [27] Here the reality of life-threatening disease overwhelms patient, physician and family and the hope for revivification is given up. Everyone is exhausted. You begin to hope the loved one will go soon. Grief is past, separation occurs, the sick child is abandoned to his fate; then unexpectedly he is lifted out of the grave. He is a stranger. Reintegration into home, family, school community comes hard.

Easson's work and the wisdom of John Donne, particularly the use of the symbol of Lazarus, point us to the moral dialectics of experimentation and submission, hope and acceptance that describe the experience of children suffering with cancer. These tensions are part of the basic life/death dialectic active in all human beings.

When we think of experimental therapeutics with children, the focus must be on values, meaning, and morals. I define experimental therapeutics as novel, unprecedented treatments which may or may not benefit the person involved or others in the future. I speak of treatments for children with life-threatening illness, treatments which carry considerable chance of benefit but also considerable risk. While ethical challenges remain great in the problems of non-therapeutic research (such as research on an aborted viable fetus) and non-invasive research (such as analysis of left-over blood and urine samples), I think that most ethically consequential research today is in the area of experimental therapeutics. I choose children because they provide what ethics has called the borderline question. Here at the borders of both scientific and moral tradition we probe questions which, when insight comes, bring clarity at the fundamental level and are generally applicable.

At the outset we need to recall the root values behind the activities of *biomedical research* on the one hand and *biomedical ethics* on the other. Both activities are born in the human impulse to help others. As with all human endeavors, these activities are morally tainted by mixed motives. Biomedical research is prompted by our desire to bring well-being to others. Of cardinal importance are the values of health and survival. Pursuit of these values is rooted in the passion to alleviate suffering. Like the Great Physician, we seek to rescue Lazarus from the jaws of death. In addition to these primary values we find secondary values such as the pursuit of knowledge and personal ambition. Together these primary and secondary values operate at the heart of that commitment of human energy and public resource we call biomedical research. The root impulse behind rebellion against disease and resistance to death is the strong claim on life as a lovely gift, and an unwillingness to relinquish it. We wish to know in order to save.

What about biomedical ethics? Here the root impulse, to use Erik Erickson's phrase, is atonement as opposed to carneval.[28] Carneval is that quality of personal and cultural animus engaging mind, heart, and will, that generates creativity, science, experimentation, the venture into the unknown. Atonement is the other pole in the dialectic, characterized by hesitancy, remorse, and withdrawal from our excursions into the unknown. Here we seek to protect and conserve values already possessed. In his great study of the Germans, Eric Kahler speaks of the sixth century Germanic warriors who ravaged the outposts of the Roman Empire then sat down and wept in remorse at their conquest. The modern spirit of biomedical ethics is born in the atoning reaction to science cut loose from personal and even human value. We live in the legacy of Nuremberg. From personal codes to institutional policies to national and international guidelines, biomedical ethics seeks to anchor, articulate and activate these atoning values. These include values such as being informed, being left alone, being protected from and compensated for injury.

The practice of medicine is shaped by the imperatives to "heal the sick" (carneval) and to "do no harm" (atonement), or, as Paul Ramsey reminds us, "to do good (beneficence) and do no evil (maleficence)." Science lives for the betterment of man, law for the preservation of man. At certain moments like the present, a strange inversion occurs. Science comes to conserve the human and personal, ethics comes to serve the abstract good. Theologically speaking, this is a time when law overwhelms grace; caution tempers conquest. Some would say that today—a day of defensive medicine and aggressive law—we actually harm people in the name of protecting them.

Sick people come to M.D. Anderson because they believe the innovative to be the best treatment and/or because all other treatments have failed. Driven by desperation and hope, they show up at Anderson as they do at Roswell Park, Sloan-Kettering and Mayo Clinic. They meet there an entourage of some of the finest scientist-clinicians in the world. Following diagnosis and lab work the patient is given the option of no treatment, standard treatment, or research investigation. In some cases those electing the traditional treatment become the control group for the research program. In the new procedures some are assigned to the test group, some to the control group. The computer often designates which patients receive which program. With some patients, historical or experiential controls are used. This means simply that the physician judges where the patient is, as a unique individual, in terms of his or her disease, and treats the patient according to intuition informed by previous experience.

What are the problems? Randomization is a profound ethical question. Let me explain. The research clinician must simultaneously hold three opinions:

(1) The experimental treatment is best.

(2) The question is still open.

(3) The new treatment may be worse than the old.

Lively debate continues as to whether our customary experimental research design—with its controls, double blinds, placebos and statistical verification—is not intrinsically unethical. Randomization will remain a necessity, required by good science and the carneval values. In clinical therapeutic research it will become more and more difficult to justify it on an ethical basis. Shoring up protection, patient advocacy, and compensation measures become an absolute necessity.

Informed consent and the full-disclosure principle are of pivotal value. They have brought much good, given the demand of scientists, including physicians, to be in complete control and unhindered. But a dangerous illusion follows if we think that fully informed consent is possible. Beecher put it succinctly: "Informed consent is not there for the asking." We need to explore what Inglefinger calls "educated consent." With children the great problem of proxy, or vicarious consent, has emerged. Fortunately we have recently discovered the amazing capacity of even young children four years old and older to participate with some knowledge in the processes of informing and consenting.

The law has sometimes forced overkill and breakdown of communication and trust. Consider the following consent form chosen at random from our protocols.

STATEMENT FOR INFORMED CONSENT FOR VELBAN-BLEOMYCIN PROTOCOL

Parent and patients will be told all the known side effects of Velban and Bleomycin. These will include granulocytopenia, thrombocytopenia, anemia, nausea, vomiting, anorexia, stomititis, weight loss, constipation or diarrhea, loss of deep tendon reflexes, paresthesias, peripheral neuropathy, constipation, hoarseness, pitosis, double vision, alopecia, fever, chills, nausea, vomiting, skin rash, hypotension, pruritis, cough, dispnea anaphylaxis and pulmonary fibrosis. In addition to all above, there may be some unknown side effects of each drug. Combination of these drugs may cause some immunosuppression resultant unpredicted serious or fatal infections.

The difficulties are evident. The doctors I work with are extremely careful at this point. They know that patients are caught up in a desperate yearning for restoration of health with mingled hope and delusion, honesty and fantasy. The physician knows that the natural human propensity to deny the tragic and heighten the hopeful is epitomized in his own perception. He does not want to fail, although ultimately in every case he must.

Often the patient or family will ask the physician, "What would you do?" When that question is asked, the physician is invited to engage the patient at a deeply human level. He should not evade the opportunity. A noted Mayo Clinic physician once told a small group of medical people, "If they open me up and cancer is spread, don't do anything. Close me up. Keep me comfortable and let me go. But I could never raise this option with a patient." The time-honored tradition among researchers of putting oneself in the experimental situation is an ethical response to the golden rule. It should be nurtured in personal and public policy.

Experimental therapeutics involves high drama. On wards where children are critically ill, deep emotions—fear, guilt, rage, hope, love—oscillate wildly between optimism and resignation. Are we doing everything possible? What about this new medicine in Mexico? Maybe we should try Laetrile. A faith healer is in town; should we go? We stumble along a rocky road, driven blindly. Dramatic breakthroughs sometimes occur, as in leukemia, Wilms Tumor, Hodgkins Disease. Today the "Lazarus Syndrome" happens more frequently. Back from the brink of death, having begun grief work and transaction of death's staging, now new problems present themselves. The child may be cured; we're not prepared for that. We must assume responsibility for people whose lives we rescue from the grave. We must be sure that restoration accompanies rescue.

The drama of clinical medicine often stimulates theatrics and charades. Think of the distancing games that patients, parents, and physicians play.

Games Patients Play:

"The doctor is too busy to be disturbed by this question."
"I should know what dyspoopsia is and what a groinocologist does; I'd appear ignorant as Archie Bunker if I asked."
"I'm brave; I can't let anyone know I'm scared."

Games Physicians Play:

"I'm very busy."
"I can't say anything that will let the patient think I'm discouraged."
"I've got to sustain her hope."
"I couldn't possibly suggest no treatment as one of the alternative approaches."

Games Parents Play:

"Obey Mother and Father and everyone bigger than you."
"Good kids take their medicine."
"We can't let her know how scared we are."

The tension between research and ethics, carneval and atonement must be maintained if there is to be a therapeutic community. In the light of this analysis let me advocate some guidelines that will aid in the moral transaction of these agonizing questions.

Absolute and total honesty is essential. Sickness in children is too great a burden to bear to have it compounded by deception, deviousness and denial. We have all seen the bitter aftermath when evasions and lies have characterized a relationship. We have also seen the blessedness of courage and comfort that develop when truth is honored. Federal guidelines, hospital educational programs, and training modules for doctors and nurses should all safeguard this total honesty.

Also, we must be very careful to honor the freedom both to consent and to refuse. The danger of rendering children "therapeutic orphans" by refusing them the opportunity to participate in research needs to be reexamined. Hypercaution in the name of human protection has the danger of limiting potential health benefits. Even in non-beneficial research, children should have the option to exercise their wishes.

Given our frightened and frantic mania to do something; given the dangerous convergence of "ravenous consumers and rapacious providers" (Ivan Illich); given the absurd tendency to stumble along thoughtlessly until death intervenes—given all these, we must reaffirm again the ancient, artful suffering and death over against the manias of medicine. The new Massachusetts General guidelines for hopelessly ill patients, the hospice movement, the growing willingness to go home and begin Brompton's Mixture—are signals of this emerging wisdom.

Finally, we must advocate and nurture humility among all who minister amid these traumas of life. Humility is essential for good science and humane therapeutics. It is only when one learns to contemplate nature, said Kepler, that one can understand nature. This is particularly true in dealing with people. Humility, earthiness, humor—it's all the same. The essence of humility is setting aside self-obsession in favor of concern for others.

Many modern writers have reflected on the moral meaning of Lazarus. These include Eugene O'Neill (*Lazarus Laughed*) and Sylvia Plath ("Lady Lazarus"). C. S. Lewis reflects on the death of his wife in *A Grief Observed*.

> What sort of a lover am I to think so much about my affliction and so much less about hers? Even the insane call "come back" is all for my own sake. I never even raised the question whether such a return, if it were possible, would be good for her. I want her back as an ingredient in the restoration of my past. Could I have wished her anything worse? Having got once through death, to come back and then, at some later date, have all her dying to do over again? They call Stephen the first martyr. Hadn't Lazarus a rawer deal? [29]

We quoted earlier the words of the English cleric, John

Donne. Another English canon, John Henry Newman, who had witnessed the anguish of life at the brink, wrote:

Lord support us all the day long . . .
until the shadows lengthen
and the busy world is hushed
and the fever of life is over
and our work is done—
Then in thy Mercy, Grant us a safe lodging,
an eternal rest—and peace at the last.

The Book of Common Prayer

Deliberate Death As Biological Adaptation

The developments in clinical medicine outlined above which necessitate more deliberate human choice express underlying movements in evolution, biological adaptation, and human progress. It is progress in biomedical knowledge and increased power over certain aspects of disease that have ushered in this new measure of responsibility.

Two provocative articles in leading scientific journals have raised the question of death election from the world of nature. Kerr L. White writes in *Scientific American:*

Should diseases be likened to ivy growing on the oak trees— or are they part of the oak tree itself? Should diseases be regarded as human analogues of defects in an internal combustion engine or a Swiss watch, or should they be regarded as psychobiological expressions of man evolving within the constraints and potentials contributed from his aliquot of societies' gene pool." [30]

In a similar vein, biologist-physician Robert Morrison draws the clinical inference:

Squirm as we may to avoid the inevitable, it seems time to admit to ourselves that there is simply no hiding place and that we must shoulder the responsibility of deciding to act in such a way as to hasten the declining trajectories of some lives, while doing our best to slow down the decline of others. And we have to do this on the basis of some judgment on the quality of lives in question.[31]

Another naturalistic perspective on the question of death calls attention to the fact that man is one organism in the scale of organisms, one stage in the food chain. Crudely put, all organisms eat and are eaten. In human history man has ascended to the top of the food chain by thwarting the efforts of creatures large and small to feed on him.

In this sense my friend David is a symbolic prototype of technological man. David, a fine young boy (six years old), was born with SCID (Severe Combined Immunological Deficiency). His body had no capacity to combat infections caused by invading organisms. Whereas most human beings host a wide spectrum of intestinal organisms living in mutually beneficial symbiosis, David has only recently exhibited tolerance to a few strains. He represents the far reach of human ingenuity in protecting life from assault. Walking to my office in the morning I see him playing in his bubble at Texas Children's Hospital. Germs cannot attack him. He has never had a cold or an infection. He also represents the ambivalence of our technical adventures. They may indeed become misadventures if we are "building without counting the cost" (Luke 14:28). Intervening premature death that offends our sensibility involves courageous choices later. One day David must venture out into the wonderful, yet vicious, sea of life.

Rationally understood, death is an indispensable part of nature. The logical consequence of human immortality would be the end of human development and evolution. An essential insight of Darwin's theoretical biology is the notion that death serves a moral function.

> The death of all living things is not only required to make room for new and better experiments in living; it becomes the directing force of the creative process. In the long run, the less satisfactory organism dies earlier and therefore has fewer offspring than do his superior contemporaries.[32]

Yet human commitments are offended by this logic. We have never accepted the wisdom of natural selection. In fact, human technical ingenuity can be seen as a direct challenge to nature's inexorable process of attrition and regeneration. Some would argue that we have inverted the process of survival of the fittest so that today the superior specimens of humanity are limiting birth, salvaging defective newborns, intervening naturally lethal diseases that limit procreation (e.g., diabetes) and prolonging debilitated life. At the same time the impoverished are procreating at a much more rapid rate.

These developments prove that the problems must be faced by human freedom and responsible action. Again the paradox: human initiatives against death must ultimately yield to the wise ebbs and flows of nature. At the same time, nature is amazingly receptive to creative human management. All interventions, therefore, should be guided by deeply reflective values.

In pondering these dimensions of our question we are forced to look at the accomplishment of medical progress in the face of the panorama of disease.

In William McNeill's provocative book, *Plagues and People,* we find the following passage:

> In 1700, Queen Anne's son and sole surviving direct heir died of smallpox. . . . Scarcely had the union of England and Scotland and the Hanoverian succession been agreed upon than another smallpox death in 1711 disastrously disrupted (political) plans. . . . These two events . . . sharply altered the course of British political history, alerted the ruling classes of the British Isles to the dangers of smallpox. This set the stage for systematic inquiry by members of the Royal Society for ways of forestalling unexpected adult deaths. . . . Organized medicine thereby began for the first time to contribute to population growth in a statistically significant fashion.[33]

The passage shows how scientific knowledge, medical practice, and political values converge against disease to give history a new well-being but also a new moral crisis. The basic rule of all human interaction in nature is that you can never do only one thing. Every action sets in motion other effects—known and unknown. Every conquest of a death necessitates another death.

The fundamental characteristic of human life is death. Disease prefigures death. Unless we see death as absurdity and consequently disease as contradiction, we must acknowledge, even within an evolutionary perspective, that disease is natural. It is nature's experiment. Religion argues that disease and death are contradictions in nature, calling us, through a sense of our contingency, to our authentic spiritual being.

Consider the following model. Man is a single warrior standing outside a castle with a thousand archers posted inside. They fire their arrows with deadly accuracy but various speeds. Companions arise to stand by the warrior. They have shields to deflect the deadly arrows. Many arrows are deflected but one eventually penetrates and kills the man. This is an allegory of man's vulnerable situation in a world where he has some protection from medicine. Many of the diseases are thwarted as they seek his life, but finally he must meet his death. The protection of medicine spares his life for the time being. Arrows representing the plagues, infant mortality, childhood infections, etc., do not penetrate his heart as they once did. Now cancer and emphysema, heart disease and arthritis, slower but equally well-armed arrows, find their mark. The individual today has some choice in selecting the arrows that will come through the defense. When the warrior is felled, when man's warfare is accomplished, he is carried into the castle.

As we seek to evaluate morally the biomedical interventions which influence disease, a philosophical approach is necessary; that is, we must survey the wide-ranging consequences and implications of our questions and procedures. To conclude this chapter, we will look at seveal areas of impending breakthrough in biomedical knowledge which help people adapt to the challenges of their internal and external environment. These scientific developments involve consequences for disease management. They also present political and ethical problems.

The Web of Life

A change in one part of the web of life creates stress in another part. But in medicine we are not only dealing with reducing disease from one cause, thereby increasing it from other causes, we are dealing with life expectancy and longevity. Reducing infant mortality increases geriatric problems and creates, at least by contrast, the happy problem of death from old age. Latest studies suggest that, in the absence of unforeseen forces, eradication of cancer will increase life expectancy 2.5 years for those under 35, 1.4 years for those 65 years of age. Significant breakthroughs in vascular disease would increase life expectancy even more dramatically—by seven years for those under 35.

Alongside this salutory perspective must be held the economic variable. Reducing deaths from sudden causes like accidents and infections necessitates endurance of more costly deaths. While sudden coronary and cerebral death may be a blessing in terms of expense, cancer and the other degenerative disorders often devastate one's personal finances.

Microorganismic Disease

After World War II, we began to use DDT as a widespread insecticide. McNeill notes that this was "one of the most dramatic and abrupt health changes ever experienced by mankind." [34] Not only did the use of DDT have profound health consequences, it also had political consequences, especially in the tropical and equatorial world. It destroyed much of the insect life as well as the large animals who fed on the poisoned insects. The effects of DDT on sea life have been painfully documented. The moral dilemmas caused by such procedures are provocative. Shall we destroy life in order to save it? Shall we inflict a greater magnitude of suffering in the present and future population by intervening now? Can we morally refrain from doing something that will alleviate present suffering and save lives? Can we not feed the famished of Bangladesh now because of what it may mean for the next generation?

Malaria is just one manifestation of the wide range of diseases caused by those tiny microorganisms that live with us. Bacteria, fungi, viruses, parasites abide within and without, living sometimes in cooperation, sometimes in lethal struggle. The generation of postwar parents who used antibiotics for every scratchy throat and low grade fever never thought of the price that would be exacted later in their children. The moral dimension also concerned justice and distribution. Immunization forces the issue of our interdependence. The World Health Organization was formed in 1948 because of the moral insight that no man is an island, that flies infecting the food of an African child affects me in my New York apartment—if not with economic immediacy certainly with a tug of the moral ligature that links our lives together. The price of coffee, to use a current issue, affects the livelihood of thousands of workers in the tropical world.

While it may be true that the age of the plagues is past there may be several latter day spin-offs. The following possibilities should keep us alert: (1) the chance of a new strain of influenza virus (swine flu); (2) an infectious organic compound becoming lethal (Legionaires Disease); (3) a new microcreature from outer space (Andromeda Strain); (4) a new animal created in DNA recombination who gets loose; (5) discovery and isolation of the viruses that may cause degenerative diseases (cancer, neurotropic viral mental disease, diabetes, multiple sclerosis, etc.).

The decline in infections and contagious diseases and the enlarged powers to prevent and control microbial disease has changed the specter of death that persons must face. Gone forever is the Victorian deathbed scene where irreversible illness finally precipitates pneumonia or another infection and the patient calls his family together, instructs them all in "the meaning of things" before he is seized by the last eruption of "the fever of life." As Joseph Fletcher suggests, "Patients do not *meet* death anymore; the end comes for them while comatose, betubed, aerated, glucosed, narcosed, sedated." [35] The ironic effects of the demise of microbial death are the creation on the one hand of more lingering death from chronic ailments and on the other hand the increase of sudden death by accidents.

Vessel Disease and Cancer

More immediate and important are developments in vessel disease and cancer. Since fewer people die from infectious diseases, vessel and heart diseases have become more prominent in our society. Not only are these diseases extremely complex, but the therapies are also multiple and multifaceted. Some hope that we will find the genetic flaws that make some people susceptible to these diseases. This might lead to genetic counseling with recommended sterilization and/or adoption. It might necessitate fetal diagnosis and selective abortion of persons with such genetic flaws. Dietary and life-style recommendation or regulation might be a course of action. A public ban on cigarettes, alcohol, perhaps even animal fats might have a dramatic effect on the incidence of vessel disease. Medical management, surgery, and partial and/or total replacement of the heart and vessel tree are now being used to salvage some extension of functional existence for afflicted persons. Stewart Wolf's famous studies of Roseto, Pennsylvania[36] suggest that genetic, environmental, and even life-style factors are not nearly as critical in heart disease as are the collapse of social solidarity and the demoralization and "despiritization of life."

Cancer has many causes. Its treatment is therefore multi-faceted and its conquest is uncertain. We are already at the point when treatments are often worse than the disease itself. All cancer treatments with the possible exception of immunological therapy are anti-life attacks. Methotrexate, for example, is an antivitamin. Public efforts fluctuate with the political winds. Breast cancer in our most admired women, especially presidents' wives, creates a flurry of response. What will be the side effects of the war on cancer? Will suicide become the last disease? Natural death laws, intended to protect against a wrongful prolongation of life, may already point in this direction.

On the other hand, is medical progress moving us toward the idyllic age where people live to ripe old age, free from disease, then die peacefully and suddenly? "We can begin to hope," writes Dr. DeBakey, "that disease is not inescapable human destiny. Although death may remain inevitable, it need not occur prematurely or be preceded by acute and protracted suffering." [37]

If this benign vision of the end result of biomedical progress is actualized, then we will need to relearn what the Church of England calls "the grace of dying well." Though this will be difficult in the midst of high powered technology, I passionately believe that the two impulses—energetic science and graceful, courageous resignation in the face of disease—are not incompatible; indeed they blend to form a thankful response to the challenge of life.

Brain-Behavior-Control/Transplantation

Medical and moral challenges should be anticipated in the realms of brain control, behavior modification, transplantation and spare-parts medicine. The necessary therapeutic skills will be both magnificent and terrifying. The temptation to exercise these gifts for political purposes will be intense. Harry Truman and Generalissimo Franco were kept alive by macabre technical manipulation for political reasons. Psychotherapy and "reeducation" are being used today in East and West. The fascination of business, industry and HEW with sociobiology and behavioral therapy is an ominous trend in our culture.

Biomathematics

The basic sciences of physics, mathematics, and chemistry have yielded unprecedented powers when applied to human biology. The ability to understand and to mimic physiologic function and to monitor and regulate vital processes has made it possible to control many of the chemically decimating forces of disease. Yet while medicine can tune and regulate these functions it cannot restore total human life; thus medicine creates for itself new political and moral dilemmas. The questions of extraordinary life-support, definition of death and the broader philosophic questions of discerning what is "natural" and "timely" death now face us. We will examine these issues in a later chapter.

Genetic Therapy/DNA Recombination

All of these developments in biology become trivial compared to the new prospects in genetics, recombinant DNA, and molecular biology. The knowledge base is just now unfolding. The basic building blocks of life, the tiny molecule genes which are the information banks of life, are being studied one by one in all their wonder and working. The technical powers are also becoming known, including (1) basic recombination and modification, (2) creating new variants of existing organisms, (3) creating new life forms, (4) offsetting deleterious qualities, perhaps many disease traits and proclivities.

What this will mean politically remains to be seen. Unfortunately, little systematic thought has been given to the great values implicit in genetics and to positive public policy that would direct this research according to the humane wisdom. Instead we have considered these researchers to be either mad scientists or benevolent despots who would label everything innovative as dangerous.

No doubt there are profound ethical ramifications to DNA research. Biohazards and leaks are the least of these worries. The profound questions are these: What does it mean for human beings to create new life forms? What kind of human life do we seek? Is disease-free existence a desirable goal even if it is achievable? Is eradication of pain a worthwhile goal? Why is hyper-superb humanity an overriding goal in these days of such inequity of basic life chance among people? What will the quest for worthy life mean for the way we regard unworthy life?

The promise of genetics to give more children a basic chance at simple well-being is one of the noblest secrets the mind of God has disclosed to the mind of man. Can the just, wise, and compassionate impulses of the divine heart be exemplified in our use of these powers? This is the ultimate question.

Three overarching moral issues emerge from this panoramic view of biomedical progress. The first has to do with social justice, the second with perceiving and valuing natural death. The third issue is caring.

1. The cruel irony of history is that as man learns how to increase human well-being through science, the number of persons who profit from these gifts is fewer and fewer. Thus we have the strange paradox of phenomenal skill at perinatal therapeutics clashing with the blasphemous wholesale onslaught on fetal life in abortion. Some few can live better, enjoy transplants and indefinite prolongation of the life span, while for the great masses infant mortality, hunger, protein deficiency, squalor and premature death are the story. "I tremble for this nation," wrote Thomas Jefferson, "when I consider the fact that God is just. His justice cannot sleep forever." The challenge to enact distributive justice with imaginative and creative socialism, and not the boredom of the welfare state, becomes the challenge.

2. We must ponder the question of what is natural or timely death. The root myth of Puritan culture that death is demonic and a force to be rooted out, needs to be transformed into the philosopher's wisdom of "a time to be born and a time to die." If personal convictions and public policies can converge on this point without one forcing the other to an unnatural point we will be most fortunate. "Man should live as long as he should," wrote Seneca, "not as long as he can." Seneca made this discovery when Nero accused him of being part of a conspiracy and commanded him to commit suicide. Seneca also questioned our compulsion to work so that we might live better, to "spend life in making provision for life." In this he was a Hebrew. For the Jew the cardinal sins are yearning for natural immortality

and remaining sad in the face of abundance. Biomedical science should now turn its attention to helping us know how to live better. More stress must be placed on prevention of disease, health maintenance, self-care—and that gracious mutuality or "self-surrender" that is really what life is all about. "Do not try to live forever," wrote G. B. Shaw in the Preface to *The Doctor's Dilemma,* "you will not succeed. Use your health even to the point of wearing it out. That is what it is for. Spend all you have before you die, and do not outlive yourself."

3. T. S. Eliot speaks of a moment to hope and not to hope, to care and not to care. "Never harm; cure sometimes—comfort always" is an ancient medical maxim. Fierce hope and grateful resignation go together. The deeper mystery of suffering is found as we abide with one another in all the grand moments of life. In all the flowering genius and miserable limitations of man we reaffirm the insight of Eliot:

> We shall not cease from exploration, and the end of all our exploring will be to arrive where we started and know the place for the first time.[38]

This chapter has sketched the way the *Intending Death* is a new phenomenon nurtured by developments in human biological evolution, the progress of medicine, and clinical therapeutics. Since human deaths occur less often in homes and more often in hospitals and research centers, biomedical and technological progress increasingly affect our living and dying. With this analysis of critical and terminal medical care before us we can now examine a more basic sociocultural process which shapes the phenomenon we are calling *Intending Death.*

III

Life Against Death:
The Legacy of Western Culture

The Morning News, *Monday, September 27, 1976:*

New York City: An elderly Chinese couple today took the proceeds from the sale of their laundry—some $100,000—ignited it into a small bonfire in their apartment (an ancient ritual investment in immortality for oneself and one's ancestors), then with their daughter leaped from their window to their death.

Sun City, Florida: Doctors gave George Beysle, a 77-year-old cancer patient, only a few days to live. His devoted wife could not bear the thought of being left alone. They called their daughter to the apartment and then sent her out on an errand. She knew something was up. While she was away, Beysle placed a mat on the floor, lay down, shot his wife, then himself, in the head. When the daughter returned, she found them in a death embrace on the floor.

January 17, 1977:

Salt Lake City, Utah: After two unsuccessful suicide attempts, Gary Gilmore has been granted his wish to die. Convicted of murder, Gilmore had begged the state to shoot him in what

51

has now become the first execution in the United States since 1967.

March 10, 1977:

Thirty-eight-year-old Sandra Ilene West died today in Beverly Hills, California, leaving her mother in Texas three million dollars on one condition. She was to be buried with a black lace gown in a San Antonio cemetery, sitting "with the seat comfortably slanted" in her 1964 red Ferrari.

Public response to such events is ambivalent. Whether the persons be renowned—like former Union Seminary President Henry Pitney Van Dusen and his wife, Elizabeth, whose suicide pact made headlines—or just common ordinary folk, we experience strangely mixed emotions. We feel sad and proud. We see the acts as horrible and courageous. We feel sympathy: Why did it have to happen this way? So young! We didn't know they were lonely. Often we feel strangely triumphant: You pulled it off, Gramp! You really pulled it off! You beat the system that says the natural way to die is under intensive care. We should not be shocked at these conflicting emotions. They are fully human. Love of life and its underlying fear of death, along with the subconscious fear of life and yearning for death, are, as we have noted, present in all people.

The seeds of the biological and technological revolution that has changed the way we experience death are found deep in the social culture in which we live. Ours has been called a heroic, progressive, success-oriented civilization. At our roots we are a people who challenge the problems of life, including suffering and death. The tools to accomplish this are scientific knowledge and technical control and manipulation. Resignation and failure are seen as incompatible with the spirit of Western culture and the destiny of Western man. From the beginning, this spirit has been one of extraordinary energy and accomplishment. It is also one of severe tension and tragedy. The yearning of mortal man for natural immortality is by definition, ambivalent.

The spirit of Western culture, which is the spirit of modern scientific medicine, is today an erratic wind that cannot sustain full-blown the sails of our technological voyage.

Distinguished scientists at the World Food Conference in Rome suggested that perhaps famine should take its course among the peoples of India and Africa. Some argue that disease has a natural place in the history of our species and should be allowed to have its play because the side-effects of the conquest might be worse than the disease itself.

Yet today's physician and scientist, indeed any human, faced with a malnourished child or a young adult dying from leukemia, cannot accept this verdict of resignation. And so the feelings of conquest and submission, of compassion and resignation war within us.

Discerning the spirit of Western culture is essential to the task of precise analysis of the current ethical questions in medicine. Unless we understand where we are coming from and where we think we are going, we are in danger of being swept along some directionless and valueless path, the end of which we do not know and may not desire.

Consider the following dilemmas: the delicate decisions requiring a balancing of almost unlimited needs against limited resources; decisions of triage and priority; decisions to impede, accelerate or merely attend a patient in the dying process. In these cases the ability to understand the conflicting values of hope and resignation is necessary to avoid two unfortunate responses. On the one hand, empathy can create a guilt that debilitates. Garrett Hardin, the distinguished biologist, has pointed up in recent papers the destructiveness of thoughtless benevolence. On the other hand, there is that repression that makes one an automaton without conscience. Those who make decisions in medicine must delicately maintain the tension between hope and resignation.

In *Young Man Luther*, Erik Erikson locates this same dialectical tension in man's nature. He speaks of the mood of the early 16th century as reflecting "mood cycles inherent in man's psychological structure." I would suggest that holding the two moods in tension is essential to the genius of our civilization, and to the sanity of any therapist at work today. Let us label the moods Nordic and Mediterranean, northern and southern.

The Nordic spirit in our consciousness is symbolized by our unwillingness to accept the necessities of nature, including death. It is characterized by the courage with which we intervene at the thresholds of life: birth and death. In Nordic mythology the gods are man's friends, fellow warriors against the fiends and monsters let loose in the creation. One day man becomes godlike in his power and inherits extraordinary abilities through his knowledge and technology. Nordic man attacks the unknown. He challenges the alien forces in nature.

The Mediterranean spirit is different. It is born in the sun of Spain, Italy, and Africa. Southern man seeks to harmonize with the rhythms and cycles of nature. In the north the Lord must cover his earth with the white death in winter lest man cut and till it year round. In the south man walks more gently and cries to the earth as to his mother. He does not rise above the earth in mastery.

We are fortunate that life has both its Nordic and its Mediterranean elements, its North and its South. In a world such as ours, the tension between these opposite impulses is necessary and should be sustained. The great questions of medical ethics can be placed within this structure, including, of course, the question of this book: Should elective death and rejection of prolonged suffering be socially accepted and professionally administered?

Here again the delicate balance between conquest and resignation must be sought. For the sake of our sanity, for the integrity of our spirit, and for the moral legacy we bequeath to the future, we have no other option.[39]

In this chapter we will reflect initially on the background of our cultural assault on death and where this puts us vis-a-vis two contemporary expressions of intended death: euthanasia and suicide. We will then turn our attention more particularly to the question of suicide, examining the economic and cultural patterns that color our present behavior. Finally we will reflect on the moral evaluation of moving toward death, both in those suicides induced by desperation and those death intentions that result from the deeper forces and patterns in our culture.

Although our culture now experiences a deep conflict between the two impulses to attack or to accept death, widespread social acceptance of suicide and euthanasia will not occur because man is constitutionally unable to acquiesce in the face of death. What will emerge from the present crisis is a wholesome practice of elective death as a necessary corrective to the excessive intrusion of life-prolonging technology which prohibits death from having its appropriate place in our life. If this thesis proves to be true, the community of hope and its institutions has the task of providing hostels where the art of dying can be practiced humanely.

Roots of Our Cultural Assault on Death

Man is free to distort his human nature by taking the life of his fellow man for the sake of expediencies, if not extermination. Yet his basic constitution as a biological and spiritual being will prohibit him from establishing a broad social practice of euthanasia. Two characteristics of the nature of man prevent any easy acquiescence in the face of death. The *biological* root is located by Dobzhansky:

> Living creatures other than man are also mortal. Man is, however, unique in knowing that he will die. Mankind, the human species, has evolved from ancestors that were not human. A being who knows that he will die thus arose from ancestors who did not know this. The appearance of this new kind of being was an evolutionary event, certainly unprecedented on earth, possibly and even probably unprecedented in the cosmos. . . . Anxiety . . . in the face of death is . . . species wide in man. . . . People consequently strive for a union with, and for relatedness to, other human beings.[40]

Dobzhansky's argument locates a basic biogenetic resistance

to death. It is related to survival instinct. It is heightened in man's ascent from the primates. His death-awareness undergoes subtle transformation from fear which motivates struggle for survival to fear that creates compassion and concern for others. Although agreement is lacking, anthropologists from Levi-Strauss to Margaret Mead say that if any human trait is universal, it is the fear of death and repulsion against killing another person.

This impulse in man seems to intensify in his evolutionary development and technological progress. The better life becomes, the more heightened his intellectual powers, the less devastating the constraints of weather and food procurement, the more man clings to life and is able to affirm the right to life in others. The troublesome exception to this point, of course, is modern technological warfare. The anonymity afforded by long-range weapons saves combatants from face-to-face struggle, which they could not endure unless either indoctrination or mental illness had changed them into killers. Instances of friendship among combat enemies who actually meet are many. The New Year cease-fire meetings of American and North Vietnamese soldiers is a case in point. Only when the ritualized political artifice of war is resumed can one take another's life with gusto.

The importance of this observation is that man has the propensity to preserve both his own life and that of his fellow man. When man, like the rats, kills his own kind with abandon, I believe it to be a violation of his nature. Yet man's free will allows him to violate his nature in this way.

The spiritual quality rendering death an enemy and an offense may be more telling. As Luther wrote:

> *Mors in homine* is in countless ways a far greater calamity than the death of other living beings. Although horses, cows, and all animals die, they do not die because God is angry at them *(irascente Deo)*. On the contrary, for them death is, as it were, a sort of temporal casualty, ordained indeed by God but not regarded by him as punishment. Animals die because for some other reason it seemed good to God that they should die.[41]

Theologically understood in Judaic-Christian tradition, death intrudes into nature. By man death came into creation. Death has a sting because it is the payoff for sin. In the innocence of primeval life, death was not there. In the new life which is being formed in the history of nature, it will not be there. Therefore, the symptoms of mortality—disease, debilitation, anxiety—are problems to be overcome.

It might be argued that this spiritual quality of man leads him to accept death easily. In our history, this has often been the case. Gibbon speaks of the joy with which the early Christians went to their death in the Colosseum. Numerous writers noted the way many Christians peacefully accepted the devastation of the plague. A more convincing explanation of these instances of abandoning life is that they show a certain intensification of apocalyptic and pietistic consciousness. The normal Jewish and Christian mentality loves life, yearns to keep it viable, and sees it in the context of stewardship.

These two characteristics of man's nature—the biological and the spiritual—synthesize into a general quality that marks the high technical civilization of North America. In this cultural history, biomedicine has been motivated by the unwillingness to accept death. Correlatives of this viewpoint are the medical commitment to preserve life and the social prohibition of euthanasia.

How have we become the society that we are? The traditional theses have argued that Western history is infused with the Judeo-Christian understanding of time and the progress of nature. It has been marked by the striving for a situation where wars will cease, animosities in nature will be resolved and the flaws in nature—disease, pain, and death—will be overcome.

Recent research has called into question this philosophy of history. It now appears that the roots of northern European and subsequently North American civilization are not as much Judeo-Christian as they are pagan. Our high-energy, future-obsessed Puritan culture, derived from the Industrial Revolution in Northern Europe, is actually quite removed from Catholicism, at least in its Latin and Mediterranean spirit. It is based more on the understanding of man and nature that are symbolized in the Nordic myths. In this consciousness which fashioned the cultures of Germany, Scandinavia, Scotland, and England, the principal image is the power and divinity of man. One thread of the tradition, best preserved in the Icelandic Sagas, is well known to us. The myth of the descent of the gods has influenced literature, science, philosophy, and the arts such as Goethe's poetry, Wagner's operas, and Bonhoeffer's theology. The vital element in the tradition is that the gods execute themselves that man may become god. He becomes the arbiter over life and death.

It is the tension between Eastern and Mediterranean and the Nordic elements in our consciousness that causes the anxiety over euthanasia today. On the one hand, as Nordic man we strive in our science and medical care to overcome the offense of death. The magnificent obsession and compulsion of modern medicine is released in this spirit. On the other hand, Jewish and Christian man knows that he is a creature, that he is dust, that his life proceeds from God and must be relinquished again to God. Rebellion and resistance against death is only the ultimate absurd egocentricity that marks his fall.

Against this backdrop we can look at the question of euthanasia. The events in biomedical ethics in recent months point up the tension between the impulses of heroism and resignation. On the side of heroism, we can list the John Hopkins cases, the impact of the right-to-life movement, and the broader life-affirming community that has questioned fetal research, and the famous cases in Maine and Houston where medical teams have overridden the desires of parents and have proceeded with treatment rather than allow a child to die. On the acceptance and resignation side of the ledger can be grouped the New Haven cases of children allowed to die, the "living will" movement, natural death acts in several states and the growing fear of many elderly that they will not be permitted to die in God's and nature's good time because of the enthusiasm of our biomedical apparatus.

As we sketch the social history that shapes our values in this area, we must ponder the consequences that would occur should this tradition be redirected. I have stated that it seems improbable that such redirection will occur. The current willingness to openly discuss euthanasia and suicide, to advocate it, indeed in some instances to practice it, seems to me a valid corrective against the force of life-prolonging technological development. Like Tithonus of Troy, or Struldbrugs in Swift's *Gulliver's Travels*, the possession of immortality soon creates the longing to die. As we will further note in our theological section, immortality without grace is a frightening thought.

Implications of a New Social Ethic vs. Euthanasia

What would be the sociological implications for North American society if there were general acceptance of euthanasia, passive and active, as a desirable behavior norm?

Perhaps our faith in God and our understanding of life as trust will so erode in the future that men and women will wish against life for death; or, worse yet, that public policies, searching for new economies, perhaps even for survival necessities, will decide that some must die. If this new ethos does form, it would certainly be couched in very pious and moral language. The quality of life would be a frequently-used phrase. We would probably even talk about death in terms of the person's own good.

Three consequences may follow. I would mention the implications for sick and malformed persons, the implications for health professionals and the implications for society at large. In each example, I will contrast the opposite danger of the unwillingness to accept death.

The cardinal value in our culture is the unique worth of each person. This value is not posited in quality of life. The sick, the poor, the downtrodden have been the special objects of our compassion and protection. As Callahan and others have pointed out, what a tragedy it would now be to cut short this recent achievement of civilized man. The burden of bearing and rearing a mongoloid child, not to mention a Tay-Sachs child, is heavy. The compensations known to Pearl Buck, Bob Cooke, and the Kennedys are given decreasing credence as our preventive knowledge develops. Few families would choose to bear the mongoloid child if this could be prevented. Serious proposals to eradicate mongolism, Tay-Sachs, sickle cell anemia, and other inherited diseases are now before us. These proposals most often involve abortion.

It is at this point that we are experiencing deep guilt and anxiety over the present legal status of abortion. I can only interpret the recent moratorium on fetal research, the abortion riders on recent welfare legislation, and the modifications of state abortion laws where the absurd retaliatory requirement is made that the late-term abortus be salvaged and brought to term, as attempts to exonerate our guilt at the massive death we have visited on innocent children, unborn and born. How strange it is that abortion has become the world's most widely practiced form of birth control at the same time as the Viet Nam slaughter of the innocents has occurred and countless children are being condemned to death by starvation in India. Technology in a sense has empowered human malice to effect this great evil.

Unless we can recover some sense of the sanctity of human life as Callahan proposed,[42] we might indeed see wholesale onslaught on the unborn, the unwanted, the malformed, perhaps even on the undesirable and unpleasant. It takes grace to posit value in the decrepit hulks of humanity lying in the back wards of VA hospitals. Only a recovery of the terror and awe felt before the holiness of God and his image in man, or a humanistic decision for decency and fairness, can rescue us from that future.

The effect of a change in our values about preserving life and inducing, even allowing death, concerns me because of what it could do to those professions we have established to care for our health. When a young physician says, "I'm only a technician," or voices the superficially more noble sentiments,

"I only carry out the wishes of the patient," or, "I can't play God," I become apprehensive. What will we have done if we compromise the preservation-of-life value in doctors either by excessive legal prohibitions or by public cynicism? What if the physician becomes a public enemy? This may be a more real threat than we think. Anger over costs, privileges, and access, is generating only higher costs, unionism, and greater protectiveness from the medical professionals. We cannot tolerate the exploitation that marks an entrepreneurial system like ours, nor can we allow the corruptions that set in when the physician is the tool of public policy.[43]

We in the United States need to learn from Canada's experience with fashioning a national health system. More important, we need to reconstitute what Paul Ramsey calls the covenant between the physician, the vitally important health system, and the society. We need to reestablish those qualities of trust, communication, fairness, and justice that alone can sustain meaning in the struggles of life and death.

For society at large the issues are more difficult. We cannot continue to increase the birthrate and the survival rate, and decrease the death rate. This is like asking time to stand still while we effect our technological ventures. It is a sin to initiate technical modifications without bearing the consequences of such innovations. For example, if we affirm the right of young children without adequate immunological response to survive, we need to establish programs and institutions to care for them. In many cases we must be prepared either to counsel sterilization or to provide facilities for offspring who will probably be retarded.

To modify our commitments on euthanasia would further erode this kind of responsibility. The main arguments for widespread euthanasia are those of convenience, economic expediency, and scarce resources.

We must learn that our transformation from innocence to knowledge is not an entree into easy life, but into life fraught with responsibility. As Niebuhr has noted, we do not get better or worse as evolution progresses; rather, our capacity for good and evil intensify. Right now we seek relief from the burdens of living and caring in our acceptance of revised norms of abortion and euthanasia. We need to look at those hard commitments which the maturing of the human race is going to demand. Then we need faith and hope to claim them within the promise that God is making all things new.

Thus far we have argued that both the hesitancy at the prospect of deliberate death and the tendency toward electing death are shaped by moral values in our cultural tradition. These values are formed by the combination of technology, economics, and religion, along with many other components of our culture.

As civilization advances, a greater proportion of the total deaths are elected, inflicted, or otherwise intended. If we divide all deaths into four groups—natural (diseases), accidents, homicide, and suicide—death from natural causes alone is diminishing. There is an even more telling trend because many deaths from disease often have human intentionality—conscious and unconscious—as part of the cause.

Although careful records were not kept and indeed are still difficult to maintain, there is little doubt that a subtle shift is occurring as man's evolution progresses. Today approximately 15% of all deaths are unexplained.[44] A large proportion of these deaths which will be formally recorded as accidents are likely intended deaths of some kind. Today, as natural deaths (deaths from disease) decrease, deaths by lethal aggression (suicide, homicide) and accidents increase. It might be argued that fewer natural deaths necessitate human initiatives in death. In any case, elective deaths (euthanasia and suicide) are classified as a part of lethal aggression.

In an extremely important study, Hugh P. Whitt and others have shown that lethal aggression varies by religious tradition and industrialization. Lethal aggression (suicide and homicide) decreases with industrialization in Protestant nations, increases with industrialization in Catholic nations. Regardless of religious tradition, increasing industrialization is accompanied by an increasing tendency for lethal aggression to take the form of suicide rather than homicide. Protestant nations show a tendency to express aggression as suicide, while Catholic and non-Christian nations have a greater tendency toward homicide.[45]

The underlying assumption of Whitt's study is that there is a pent-up aggressive energy in individuals and populations caused by frustrations, role conflicts, and the like. These energies erupt either into external conflicts (i.e., wars, economic imperialisms), or into internal expressions of destructive behavior. They can also be sublimated or projected (it may be presumed) into artistic creativity or spectator sports. Max Weber [46] argues that Protestantism pushes men into economic pursuits. Striving for creativity, productivity, the accumulation of capital, and economic vitality are elements of the view of time and nature implicit in the cultural revolution associated with the names of Martin Luther and John Calvin. In contrast to the Eastern faiths which are otherworldly—stressing escape, resignation and apathy —this faith is worldly and political. Leonard Berkowitz suggests that within this milieu persons who are masters of their own fate must blame themselves for their failures and frustrations,[47] thereby internalizing lethal aggression.

Within the Weber tradition, Emile Durkheim has written the first great Western social analysis of suicide.[48] In this study he shows how Protestantism nurtures the autonomous, self-sufficient person who sees life in terms of personal initiative.

Western men and women, while still eager for longevity and and obsessively afraid of death, actually are so consumed with self-destructive behaviors that the fundamental love and stewardship of life is undermined. We bomb villages in order to save them. We pollute all that we eat, drink, or breathe. Some even suggest that it is now dangerous for mothers to breast-feed their newborn because their milk might contain carcinogenic substances because of pesticides. Our life-style is both sedentary and frantic. We reward and reinforce sickness while punishing health. We pick up the slack for persons who don't feel well. We expect more and more from one who is well. In America, sickness and suicide rise and fall directly with economic indicators and unemployment. Most suicidal behavior is subtle, perhaps even subconscious. It expresses itself in diets, drugs and exercise, not fastening seat belts, and in generally living dangerously. The numerous stress-related diseases which come when life-changes disrupt equilibrium are often symptomatic of an underlying carelessness.[49]

Our Western society has conceived itself as a warrior/aggressor/redeemer people. In the name of life it has spread death. Seeking peace and order we have precipitated violence and disorder. Today in the service of health we inflict great suffering on people. When all is said and done, persons who have undergone cancer chemotherapy, surgery, or radiation often wonder whether it was really worth it. The technological preservation of physical life may cruelly distort human life and destiny. The specter of Karen Quinlan is unimaginable and indeed impossible in the age before the artificial respirator, intravenous and nasogastric tube feeding. We are driven again to our moral and spiritual heritage to call into question what we are doing and to discover again the way we should go.

Meditation: *Acquisitiveness, Energy, Anxiety and Aversion to Death*

The strong Lord says, "the day is coming when proud and evil people will burn up like straw, there will be nothing left of them. But for you who obey me, my saving power will rise on you like the sun and bring healing like the sun's rays. You will be free and happy as calves let out of a stall. On that day when I act, the wicked will collapse like dust under your feet. Remember the teachings of Moses, the laws and commands were given at Sinai for my people Israel to obey.

But before the great and terrible day of the Lord comes I will send Elijah, my prophet. He will bring fathers and children together again. Otherwise I would have destroyed the land" (Malachi 4:1-6, my translation).

These words draw to a close the Hebrew Bible.

Sunday, March 6, 1977

As dawn broke across the hills of eastern Pennsylvania this morning, Ronald Adley climbed up from his tomb. For a week he lay in a cold dark cell deep inside the mountain near Tower City. He had scrambled there after a tide of water broke through the wall of the coal mine. That was Tuesday. Wednesday his tapping on the wall was heard and a thin shaft was drilled. This became a life-line where food, drink and sustaining words could be piped down. At this very hour persons lie entombed under the earthquake rubble in the environs of Bucharest. Some will be reached or crawl out, others will not! When nature crushes in on us, we are brought to a confrontation with life's meaning. This night your soul is required of you—face to face with death and perhaps rescue, judgment and perhaps joy.

On Friday I said goodbye to Laurie—a lovely fifteen-year-old blonde from Missouri. On Thursday the doctors had told her that nothing else could be done for the cancer on her neck and jaw. Nearly a year had passed since they first discovered the nodule. In and out of M.D. Anderson—month after month—surgery, chemotherapy, loss of hair, constant nausea, disfigurement, pain, hope, disappointment, $200,000 in bills (the last treatment being 14 grams of methotrexate at $14,000 a bottle). Now the long drive back to Missouri to wait for the inevitable! The fear of death and the fight for life have brought depth of meaning, a sense of gratitude and generosity to this family in the midst of profound sorrow. "How's your wife, Sara? How's your little girl?" she asked me as they drove off. "If your new baby is born on May 24, be sure to name her Laurie!"

The words of Malachi—the last words of the Old Testament—speak to us in the crisis of impending death. "The strong Lord says . . . ."

Paul Tillich has a sermon in *Shaking of the Foundations* which tells of a refugee from the law who hides for years in the stench of an animal pit. One day he is lifted out into the light, into the fresh air—into forgiveness. Each of us has a rendezvous with our destiny—a crisis of awareness—a dark night or a bright day when things are made plain. Texans call it a showdown. The truth of things can penetrate in agony or ecstasy, and our being is transported momentarily from the mundane by crisis. This crisis can throw us in one of two directions: towards salvation, which his freedom, sacrifice, openness, generosity, and responsibility; or towards damnation, which is bondage, protection, closure, self-service and neglect. Life is a sequence of such moments—showdowns, second chances. How do we respond to the fear of death? Do we react in neurosis, becoming impersonal, obsessive, frivolous? Or do we welcome the fracture in our lives as the window of grace, letting us see what it takes to become passionate, sympathetic, and serious about life?

The Bible says we choose this day whom we will serve—mammon or Jehovah, comfort or challenge, frenzy or peace. We can choose death or life. Most of our choices are for security and death. Yet his grace hounds us to the ends of the earth. The Hebrew word for grace mimics the cry of a mother camel in the desolate sands of the desert, crying for her lost calf; *grace:* amazing, seeking the lost, rescuing us from the snares of death.

Fear of death sends us on either the risky pilgrimage of faith or the flight of denial. Look at the values that constitute the flight of denial. Think of acquisitiveness and the energy crisis, and how these are related to the fear of death. There is a syndrome of life evasion. It blends these three elements: (1) acquisitiveness, the will to possess and consume, (2) the energy crisis, our urge to overindulge and hoard, and (3) death aversion, whenever we refuse to accept boundaries. These traits grow like branches from a single root.

A wise psychiatrist has written: "It is ultimately the fear of death which is behind our craze to acquire, possess and incorporate, behind our greed and sadism and the predatory aspects of our modes of life." [50] Let us diagnose this syndrome and then receive the prescription of the Gospel. When we speak of acquisitiveness we speak of a personal and collective obsession which craves things, yearns for affluence—a disposition which takes from life with no thought of replenishment. It finds great difficulty in feeling responsible for what one does. It senses no obligation to future generations. It tacitly approves violence, aggression and corporate evil in the name of keeping things composed and orderly. The mentality seeks to isolate, insulate, and to build up layers of things. It seeks to possess—and if the fascination with *The Exorcist* means anything—it seeks to be possessed, to be owned, to feel life owes you a living. Persons are commodities to be bought and sold, used and disposed of— recycled maybe—but only if the new product is usable. Fromm calls the syndrome the "mechanization of life"—seeing persons as functions. Buber spoke of it as configuring life in an I-It rather than an I-Thou relationship.

All in all it is a desperate escape from freedom—a fear of interdependence and responsibility; a frantic effort to avoid facing life in its terror and joy.

Young and old are afflicted. It is the disease of the teenage mechanics in *Zen and the Art of Mortorcycle Maintenance*, who are no different from incompetent doctors or from disabling teachers. While his bike is being reduced to a scrap heap by the young servicemen, the author reflects:

> The biggest clue seemed to be their expressions. They were hard to explain. Good-natured, friendly, easy-going—and uninvolved. They were like spectators. You had the feeling they had just wandered in there themselves and somebody had handed them a wrench. There was no identification with the job, no saying "I am a mechanic." They were outside of it, detached, removed. They were involved in it, but not in such a way as to care.[51]

Our acquisitiveness, our anxiety at the energy crisis, and our aversion to death are characteristics of our attempt to hold back the trauma of the new day dawning and its responsibility to care.

Let's take a closer look at acquisitiveness. Dow Jones indicators replace clocks on the towers of our buildings. This becomes the significant measure of our life. Norman Mailer talks of the shimmering madonna called the Apollo Rocket. The vehicle assembly building is our cathedral. We not only have tall silos and elevators with food for humans and cattle, but also underground silos with other "gifts," which are directed at our enemies. C. S. Lewis describes this modern nest-fowling technomania when he introduces Professor Weston in *Out of the Silent Planet:*

> He was a man obsessed with the idea . . . that humanity, having now sufficiently corrupted the planet where it arose, must at all costs continue to seed itself over a larger area . . . (those) vast astronomical distances which are God's quarantine regulations. This for a start. But beyond this lies the sweet poison of the false infinite—the wild dream that planet after planet, system after system, in the end galaxy after galaxy, can be forced to sustain everywhere and forever, the sort of life which is contained in the loins of our own species—a dream begotten by the hatred of death upon the fear of true immortality.[52]

Our public paranoia is of course our personal fear writ large. We each have in our heart a fear: of exposure, of isolation, of cold, of darkness, of death. The suburban experience is one that seeks to isolate and insulate life from the urban anguish. The protective process is one of building homes, acquiring goods, boats, lake properties, etc. In the end the acquisitive process is an attempt to deny one's mortality. Elisabeth Kübler-Ross has noted that the affluent die hard. The poor find it easier to die well and to care. We try to convince ourselves that we won't die. The result is alienation. Youth estrangement, with all the special indicators (runaways, drugs, depression, violence), increases in direct proportion to the affluence and acquisitiveness of the community.

Karl Marx, when he was most attuned to the Hebrew prophets, wrote, "the devaluation of the human world increases in direct relation with the increase of value in the world of things." [53]

The energy crisis is a primeval signal of our mortality. When cave man's fire went out he knew he would die. In 1977, the ice age in the North and the drought in the West did not bring new experiments in conviviality or technological imagination. Rather these crises only nurtured the cry for more—more energy, more jobs, more houses, more indulgent paternalism. Our response to natural crisis has gone from hedonism to stoicism. "Eat, drink and be merry, for tomorrow we die" is giving way to the ascetic view "all things in moderation; although we may die our resignation will be heroic." The crisis could indeed have had the good effect of drawing us to home and hearth, to a clinging to each other to keep warm. This may indeed generate a new frugality, and enhance life-awareness, but I fear it will be short-lived because of our passion for progress. Our acquiring and consuming instincts control our national and international life. Don Shriver states:

> We have for at least 200 years—during all of American history —reasoned socially from the psychology of poverty. Scratch most Americans, and you find the fear of going back to the poverty of their ancestors. Hence the compulsive pursuit of wealth in America by individuals, corporations, society as a whole.[54]

Herman Daly, the brilliant economist at Louisiana State University, writes:

> The original sin of infinite wants has its redemption vouchsafed by the omnipotent savior of technology, and that the first commandment is to produce more and more goods for more and more people—world without end.[55]

The primary ethical significance of the energy crisis is that of boundary, limitation. In that sense, it is a precursive symbol of our death.

Aversion to death is the element in our experience that most seriously prevents us from enjoying life. Freud called death the final castration and narcissistic insult. The grotesque fantasies that grow from our denial of death are all around us: on the screen, in books, in music. We fear not only the death at life's end but also the daily deaths necessary to growth—the throwing off of the old which growth requires. Tragedy, pain, suffering, bearing another's burden, listening—all of these are exercises in letting go which alone allow growth and healing, and we avoid them like the plague.

To watch and pray in the garden of death is too difficult.

We go to sleep. Biblical religion understands this agony and speaks forcefully to it. It sees our acquisitiveness, our power failure, and our death aversion, and it seeks to heal us, to make us real men and women.

> Do not put aside for yourselves valuable things on earth which rust away and lure the robber; but put your treasure where God is, where there is incorruption. Where your possessing love is, there is your will, your heart. Care not for the body, nor the morrow; its own evil is sufficient (Matthew 6, my paraphrase).

If this analysis is accurate, a revolution in belief and behavior is required if we are to survive, let alone survive with meaning and happiness. The conclusion seems clear. We must live with abandon, which is joy. We must live carefully—building and governing this world as priests, kings and prophets. We must live as technologists—as gardeners, replenishers, as motorcycle maintainers. We are to laugh at death, because its sting is gone; not its fear nor its pain, but its claim on us. Jesus Christ came into the earth—descended into hell—and led captivity captive in himself.

In 1905 Gustav Mahler wrote the famous song cycle *Kindertotenlieder*. These songs on the death of children reflect his attraction to life even in the midst of death. The final song completes the cycle:

> In this weather, in this awfulness, I would never have sent the children out. They were dragged out. I was not allowed to say anything against it. In this weather, in this storm, in this shower, they are resting, resting, as if they were at home with mother. Frightened no more by storms, watched over by God's hand, they are resting, as if they were at home with mother.

> (Translation, William Mann, 1959) [56]

The final cultural dimension of death perception and response is found in those studies that show that persons think about it differently at various stages in the life cycle. The child sees death as a metamorphosis, a going away. Children who are dying of cancer, or who are reflecting on the death of a friend, will often use a symbol prevalent among the Greeks—the cocoon and butterfly. For the child between one and three, death means to depart. Existence goes on in another form in some other place.

From ages five to nine, the idea of personal death begins to take shape. The pre-adolescents I have known at M. D. Anderson develop a remarkable realism and courage as they go toward death. They often become centers of strength for families and medical teams who are themselves at wits' end. The pre-adolescent still has the magic of a childlike faith.

In puberty and adolescence one has started to invest in one's world. There are girlfriends and boyfriends, acne, and stereo records. Peer awareness becomes strong and one is offended at having to disengage from the lure of life that is so filled with excitement. At this period of life, self-development and the promise of the future are vivid. It has been my impression that young teenagers with terminal prognoses do come to peaceful acceptance of their fate after an intense and courageous effort to live. It is interesting to observe teenagers who go into remission and may indeed be "truly cured." [57] While they develop this remarkable maturity and strength in the face of a grim prognosis, when they are reprieved from impending death they tend to become just as faddish, selfish, and distracted as any other teenager.

One poignant exception deserves mention. In our culture, as was previously noted, we reward sickness and punish health. When a young person has cancer, the parents and siblings will often bend over backwards not to offend him, not impose on him, nor ask him to do anything strenuous. In other words, normal behavior is altered. Sick boys or girls often wish that others would treat them like anyone else. They might say, "Be yourself;

be mean!" Sometimes being shouted at to take out the garbage
can be therapeutic to a critically ill young person. But if prefer-
ential treatment continues, those who pamper often grow weary
and subsconciously come to wish that death would intervene and
"get it over with." In the Lazarus Syndrome premature disen-
gagement can take place so that the then-dying/now-well individual cannot be reintegrated into family, school, community. This
special category of the "sick role" that our culture has created for
the ill is often a condemnation to death masquerading as concern.

The teenager in permanent remission from leukemia, for example, goes home and back to school. His development and normal interactions have been grotesquely misconstrued during his
years of treatment and hospitalization. When he goes back home,
the family is not prepared for his resurrection. At school he is
out of place. He has lost his hair; he probably has permanent
gonadal injury from the treatment, and the kids think he is infectious. This new phenomenon is going to present a profound
challenge to our cultural perceptions and values regarding death
and life. If we are going to snare someone back from the jaws
of death, we need to be sure we really want to and are prepared
to reclaim and reintegrate the rescued ones with all the cost and
discipline which that entails.

As one matures death becomes a threat to family stability.
A man worries about what will happen to his wife and children
without a provider. Here one's religion determines the differ-
ences in reaction. Some may choose repression and denial; others
may slowly prepare for the inevitable.

Thomas Hardy reflects on the contemporary age and paints
the plight of "unnoticed" man in his 1890 novel, *Jude the Obscure*. Jude and Susan have just discovered the lifeless bodies
of their children hanging in the chamber room of the inn where
they are staying. Their son, Jude, has left a note saying, "we are
too many." Susan blames herself because she spoke with young
Jude of the additional burden of a new child on the way.

"No," said Jude. "It was in his nature to do it. The doctor says there are such boys springing up amongst us—boys of a sort unknown in the last generation—the outcome of new views of life. They seem to see all its terrors before they are old enough to have staying power to resist them. He says it is the beginning of the coming universal wish not to live." [58]

Hardy had prophetically foreseen the terrible depersonalization and anonymity that characterize technological society. Unless life is imbued again with mystery and meaning, deaths will be statistics evoking neither anguish nor gratitude and peace. Love of life is a belief. To sustain the will to live requires belief and being believed in. When one has no reason to get up in the morning there is the serious question of how resistant one will be to a beckoning illness. The social factors—family, neighborhood, town and nation, and the values and investments these entities place in persons, influence the life/death tension in profound ways.

In this chapter we have noted the social forces that take the scientific and clinical elements of our culture and blend them into a framework of understanding that guides the way persons think about death. Our cultural history is characterized by the same tension that we found in our analysis of the biological and clinical situation. We now turn to the area where constructive social thought attempts to grapple with this ambivalence in its attempt to speak of "natural" and "timely" death.

IV

Natural and Timely Death

An act relating to the Natural Death Act and a procedure for a person to provide in advance for the withdrawal or withholding of medical care when the person has a terminal condition.

(Texas Senate Bill 148, 1977)

"We regret the untimely death of our colleague," eulogized a medical professor. "It teaches us how much we have yet to learn in science."

(A Medical Newsletter)

EIGHTEENTH CENTURY PHILOSOPHERS—inspired by the new-found human powers of reason and technical mastery over nature, offended by the forces and institutions that restricted man's possibility—dared to dream a dream that had not crossed the human mind since the early Christian era. It was the dream of "natural death." This benevolent death would come only after all the vital forces of being were exhausted. In his *Outline of the Progress of the Human Mind,* Condorcet anticipates that day when death

will be nothing more than the effect either of extraordinary accidents, or of the slow and gradual decay of the vital powers;

75

and that the duration of the interval between the birth of man and his decay will have itself no assignable limit. Certainly man will not become immortal; but may not the distance between the moment in which he draws his first breath, and the common term, when in the course of nature, without malady, without accident, he finds it impossible any longer to exist, be necessarily protracted? [59]

Other romantics were even bolder than Condorcet. They dreamed of an indefinite prolongation of the human life span here on the earth. Evoking arguments found in the Greek fathers of the church, persons like John Asgill claimed that the covenant of eternal life revealed in the Scriptures would be realized as man's knowledge and power (which was identical with divine dominion) enlarged in the earth. Needless to say, Asgill was removed from his seat in parliament and his writing censured.

The paradoxical quality of death—coming as it does in the prime of life—contradicts the view that the wisdom built up in a person should not be extinguished. Death offends our idea of justice. It brings grief to the human family. This offense has always enticed the human mind to imagine circuitous routes around the harsh reality. Of all the creatures, man alone knows that he will die, yet is unwilling to believe in the finality of death. Prompted by this ambivalence, he invests tremendous energy delaying the inevitable. We search for deaths that might be called "natural" or "timely" and the assault on "unnatural" and "untimely" deaths is an attempt of the human spirit to accept the inevitable while not laying waste to our hope.

Today we seek to define and defend "natural death" in public policy, medical practice, scientific initiatives, and personal decisions. To say that death is a natural part of life is a new realistic viewpoint, reflecting the relaxing of certain culturally ingrained denials and manias. But it also reflects a turning from our Judaic heritage toward the Greek world view. This latter point will be examined in the next chapter. In this chapter we will look at (1) the modern development of the idea of "natural" or "timely" death as a dimension of materialistic philosophy, (2) the various shades of meaning which "natural death" and cognate notions have taken on, and (3) the constructive meaning of this quest as we search for good deaths. Reflections on the experience of the Karen Quinlan family and the Church of England report on "Dying Well" will conclude this section.

We are attempting to support our central thesis that paradox and contradiction is the fully human response to death and that human initiatives in death and dying are only safe if this root tension is safeguarded. The practice of rationalizing death is universal. Attempting to satisfy ourselves that the death of a person we know is natural or timely is perhaps the classic form of this rationalization. The danger comes when we fail to recognize our rationalizations for what they are.

Instance: the phone rings. It is Johnny, your friend down the street. A woman you both know from church has just collapsed from a coronary attack. Your first question: how old was Mary? Sixty-eight. Oh! I didn't know she was that old. The first question may be different. Did she have any history of heart disease? She had some angina, and she never let it bother her and never went to the doctor. Oh! I understand.

Here we have two highly typical responses to death. The initial shock and disbelief evokes these two generic questions, which are designed to test whether the death was timely or natural. If we can gain some satisfaction that it was either timely or natural we rest in the fact that we have somehow absolved the absurdity and made it easier to accept. Again, these all become attempts to unscrew the inscrutable. The death of children is always particularly offensive. It is hard to comfort oneself that deaths in children are ever timely and hardly ever natural.[60] Sometimes when the infant has a fatal flaw (a birth defect, for example), we can see the inevitability—perhaps even the desirability—of death.

When there is a built-in error, death—however absurd—becomes the logical working-out of some lethal system and it is somehow acceptable. We may even say: "It was the best"; "God took him from us"; "His appointed time had come." But most often death in children devastates not only our rational systems but our moral vision of life as well. As Dostoevsky's Ivan Karamazov said, it becomes a scandal and a sufficient reason for atheism.

Evolution of the Natural Death Concept

The search for natural or acceptable death is an ancient one. Indeed the entire history of thought could be examined by posing the tension between those philosophers who find death acceptable, even noble (Socrates)—and those who see glory in man's struggle against death, his rising in mastery over life and death, including his own. Contemporary Marxism, like the Enlightenment and the flowering of Greek and Roman humanism, argues that death is bondage and defeat. Man should aspire to that natural death which is not dictated by fate or by the will of others. The root notion behind this belief is that man deserves immortality. He is master in the earth. Natural evolution and reason decree that he should rise above necessity and strain toward a universal immortality. Man should struggle to defeat accidental deaths (through technical manipulation of environment), deaths from impoverishment (through regeneration of the socioeconomic order), and from human malevolence (by ridding the state of the exploitative forces of greed and coerced labor.)

In the materialistic and dialectic versions of modern philosophy, man must "rage against the dying of the light." But Dylan Thomas' existential pathos is not enough. There must also be deliberate counter-efforts to forestall and prevent death. Herbert Marcuse argues that man ought always to react toward death with a "great refusal." Science rightly used in the service of life will bring the benefits of longevity. This will be achieved through power over the forces of death before which man has heretofore stood helpless.

The gradually increasing duration of life may change the substance and character not only of life but also of death. The latter would lose its ontological and moral sanctions; men would experience death primarily as a technical limit of human freedom.[61]

Blending the notions of Judaism and Marxism, Ernst Bloch argues that since death is inescapable, man must struggle to leave landmarks of beauty, justice and knowledge so that he lives on through his works. The person who is able to rise above class consciousness and individualism is enabled to overcome anxiety and alienation and receive death with equanimity, knowing that he has woven himself inextricably into the fabric of life.

Bloch argues that death does not destroy but rather brings into actualization the creatively new in the human story. "In the content of death there is no longer merely death but the uncovering of life-content that has been gained." [62]

Natural death in this modern interpretation thus becomes death without anxiety. Because of technology and social reform, today's death caused by human squalor, exploitation, meaningless toil, disease, and accidents will gradually yield to natural death.

There is great strength in this thought. But the materialism of modern scientific philosophy leads it into a dangerous collapse of the tension and the result is a simplification. T. W. Adorno writes:

> In view of the potential of control over organic processes, a potential of which the outline is becoming visible, the idea of the abolition of death cannot *a fortiori* be disposed of.[63]

W. Fuchs sees the presentation of guarantees of old age in biomedicine as the essence of its quest for "natural death." Even now society possesses potentialities for "making itself in ever growing measure the master of death." [64]

A thoroughgoing materialistic world view will collapse the tension between life affirmation and death acceptance. It does so in one of two ways. On the one hand it hopes to prolong life indefinitely. Most often, when this optimism collapses, resignation sets in. Here it is argued that since decay and death reign in nature man must give in and not resist. Guardini sees this capitulation as the dangerous legacy of scientific materialism.

> In recent years acceptance of death has largely taken on a form that can be characterized as nothing other than capitulation. Man has to a great extent given up his protest against death because he can no longer bear the constitutive conflict, as it might be called . . . ; this has taken place in closest connection with the biologization and socialization of existence. . . .[65]

In this light acceptance of death can be seen as the inevitable consequence of a world where belief has faded, where God is dead, where hope is gone. Resisting death and cherishing life are expressions of the religious world view. The search for natural death, while a necessary corrective against a futile grasping at vitality, cannot undergird a public policy or personal philosophy. Such would seek at once to remain true both to the right to life and the rightness of death.

In a letter of October 17, 1651, to his sister Gilberte, Blaise Pascal, on the occasion of the death of their father, wrote:

> We should not look at death like pagans, but as Christians, that is with hope, for this is the special privilege of the Christians. We should not look at the corpse as deceptive nature shows it to us, as a putrefying piece of flesh but as the inviolate and external temple of the Holy Spirit. . . . The mistake of philosophers is to consider death natural to man. This is a childish and base view. For man as animal is born and dies, and death, according to the laws of nature, leads to the total destruction of the body. But man is created by God so that he should live with Him, and as such man does not die. Death must be seen in this perspective, and the believer has the extraordinary advantage of knowing that in reality death is punishment imposed for having sinned, and necessary for man in order for him to be able to expiate his crime.[66]

In a mood of similar French nature mysticism, Gabriel Marcel argues that whereas in materialism the cadaverization of life takes place in the view that maintains the tension of death's mystery, we affirm the consecration of life.

What I have seen clearly this morning is the fundamental am-
biguity of what I call *my life,* whether I consider it as a sequence of moments and events or whether I see it as something which is susceptible of being "given away," sacrificially,
or lost.[67]

In another place Marcel says that to love a person is to say:
"You shall not die."

At the heart of the Christian message is that pivotal event of
death that is life. At the heart of the Christian vocation is the
foolish wisdom that affirms: "In dying we live." In the light of
this wisdom the telling question becomes: Why did one die?
How did one die? Death cannot separate one from the embrac-
ing love of Christ (Romans 8:35). The critical question is how
one is found as he or she dies. This is what Christian thought
has called dying in grace or being found in Christ.

Variations of the Notion of Natural Death

This brief critique of the secular notion of natural death leads
us to the point where we can now profitably look at the notions
of natural death that function in Western culture.

The impact of Elisabeth Kübler-Ross' popular study on the
stages of dying and the effort of many states to pass "Natural
Death Acts" is not coincidental. Both movements manifest the
classic Greek notion that death is not unequivocally bad, that it
is natural, predictable, and therefore acceptable.

The world view that undergirds these efforts contends that
death is not ultimately an evil thing because it is merely the
immortal soul departing the physical body. This view will be
critically examined in a later chapter on death and immortality.

In the Marxist nations, as we have previously noted, an understanding of natural death has arisen which argues that natural
death is the free death that comes at the end of a life that has
been protected from the caprice of premature deaths caused
by acts of exploitation, alienation or immature scientific technology. Through the introduction of a philosophy of scientific

materialism and the removal of class and economic exploitations we can free more persons to die natural rather than tragic deaths.

Shneidman has introduced the related designation of "premature death." This is death that comes before one's period of productivity has ended, before one has completed their life's work, before goals have been accomplished. The dying of children and young adults strike us as particularly tragic or cruel because life is snatched at the very moment of its flowering.

Yet who is to say that the work of a three-year-old child who dies is incomplete? Pastoral comfort down through the ages has always held forth the possibility that such a person has had a rich and complete ministry even in a few short years. The idea that some deaths are premature is too frequently based on a view of life wherein value is weighed in terms of accomplishment and productivity. Theistic and some humanistic valuations will argue that such quantitative measurements are essentially shallow criteria upon which to gauge a life as complete or fulfilled.

Richard Bailey expresses this persuasion in economic terms:

> Several important points must be considered when we speak of death, particularly in relation to age and economic and social position. Age, alone, is especially significant. A person dying in his 20s, 30s or 40s has embodied with him a substantial amount of capital investment made by his family and society. Economic valuations of such persons tend, therefore, to be high and expenditures made in their behalf either by the individual or society to reduce the probability of premature death are likely to have a high payoff. In many respects, society acts quite rationally in providing health services for this age group through company-paid fringe benefits. Of course, society also exhibits just the contrary behavior in its willingness to freely expend the lives of its young men in wars.[68]

This view of death as the end of one's productive ability, as well as death seen as absurdity by poets and artists, is unacceptable to those who see death from the viewpoint of Divine

Providence. Writers in the Calvinist tradition agree that death, however seemingly absurd, is always patterned and meaningful. There is an overarching plan that informs the life of each creature that inevitably and inexorably works itself out. It cannot be derailed or cut short. It can grieve us who remain with painful loss, but even this is purposive and redemptive, working together with all things for good (Romans 8:28).

Writing in this tradition, Thornton Wilder tells the story of a bus accident on the Bridge of San Luis Rey.[69] Here on a fateful evening, many persons are killed in what appears to be an absurd and capricious mishap. Wilder then asks whether each death, rather than an absurd interruption, was rather the end of some complex ravelled story that was now in some sense complete. Being in that vehicle at that time was the logical outworking and culmination of each person's life course. The theological traditions that stress providence as the divine mode of governing life will not allow any death to be called untimely, premature, or unnatural. From the human side of the equation the deaths may seem absurd. From the divine side they punctuate personal stories that cannot and will not be thwarted in any ultimate sense.

In light of this sketch of the search for appropriate death, let us analyze a recent variation of the search for natural death. Let us examine the Natural Death Acts emerging in many states.

Natural Death Acts

Tuesday, June 28, 1977. North Carolina today became the eighth state to enact a Natural Death Law. Following California in October 1976, some forty state legislatures have considered "right-to-die" bills. Inspired by the wide public attention given to the Karen Quinlan case in New Jersey, these bills address the double bind in which physicians find themselves at the point of their patients' life conclusion. Where litigation can be initiated for acting or failing to act (i.e., suit for wrongful prolongation of life), and where there is growing advocacy and self-determi-

nation on the part of laypersons not to have life artificially prolonged, political bodies have enacted these statutes.

"Effective Friday," writes the *Charlotte Observer*, "you will be
able to determine whether you want your life prolonged by extraordinary means, such as artificial respirators." A cautious law,
it bends over backwards not to condone positive or negative
euthanasia. "No part of this law shall be construed to authorize
any affirmative or deliberate act or omission to end life other
than to permit the *natural* process of dying." The law specifically
recognizes that one's rights "as a citizen of this state include
the right to a peaceful and *natural* death." [70]

The Texas Act (S.B. 148) stresses the same points. The principal thrust of the bill is to enable persons who so desire to
have medical care withheld or withdrawn when one is in a
terminal condition. The bill protects those who have made such
"living will" affirmations from having their wishes overridden
by relatives or physicians when they, for example, have lost
powers of decision and communication. Like the California
statute, the law has careful stipulation forbidding euthanasia
and retains freedom for the individual to void this wish at any
time.

What are the virtues and potential vices of these laws? The
general strength is found in the long-needed correction to the
tendency of medicine to justify any act at any cost which pre-
serves some modicum of physical existence. In the same way
that Elisabeth Kübler-Ross has helped correct previous exces-
ses of death aversion, so these laws balance the resistance to
death and receptivity to death in its good time.

Of greater concern are the weaknesses and potential dangers
of these laws. It has been said that exotic cases make bad laws.
These statutes, provoked by Karen Quinlan type cases, will need
to be modified and refined as we gauge the actual effects they
have on persons' lives and decisions. "Those who appreciate law
or sausage," said a wise jurist, "should see neither being made."
Forming sound law is an involved, messy process.

Several critiques have been offered which deserve careful attention. Ivan Illich has argued that the Western cultural idea of natural death has evolved through four stages and is now entering a fifth stage which has some ominous implications. He analyzes these mutations during the past 500 years. First there was the "skeleton man." This way of seeing death abandoned ancient Christian notions which saw death as apocalyptic or angelic visitation. It began to visualize death as a personal skeletal specter that accompanied every person relentlessly until death brought final embrace. Using Hans Holbein woodcuts as symbols, Illich notes "the representation of each man entwined with his own death has turned into a natural force dragging all into the whirl and then mowing them down." [71]

Death was seen to be natural in succeeding centuries when it occurred as the timely death of the aging lecher, death under the critical eye, union demands for natural death, and finally death under intensive care. This modern notion of natural death is problematic because "medicine has become the dogma around which the structuring ritual of our society is organized." [72] Under the impact of industrialization and the professionalization of basic needs services, we have come to expect natural death as heroic struggle against lethal forces in high-technology, medical research centers. Where else can we do "everything possible?"

The critique Illich might bring to Natural Death Acts from this basic argument would be the question of what these laws might do to people given this underlying sociocultural value. Would those who have *not* recorded "living wills" be legally forced to endure all the ministrations of modern intensive care medicine? Will we slowly codify all decisions at death's threshold so that court orders are required for anyone to die? Will we further violate personal autonomy so that all profound life choices are bureaucratized?

Karen Lebacqz is a gifted young theologian and member of the National Commission for the Protection of Human Subjects in biomedical and behavioral research. She has served in the Health Policy Office of the state of California. In relation to the

California Natural Death Act (Assembly Bill 3060, Keene) she has argued [73] that while the act does enhance the freedom of competent adult persons to record a non-prolongation of "terminal life" document, it may prove to engender only more fear, caution, and stalling by physicians who are so threatened by the scrutiny and hegemony of law that they will actually cause sick persons prolonged terminal suffering. The bill may actually engender the opposite effect from the one desired.

Richard McCormick and Andre Hellegers of the Kennedy Institute argue that "Living Will" laws tend to restrict both patient and doctor rights. In a very thoughtful article in *America,* they write:

> To underresuscitate a patient with a living will may lead to his death, but it is unlikely to lead to a penalty since it is against overtreatment that the will is directed. Conversely, to overresuscitate a patient with a will and to leave him in a state repugnant to him may save his life, but makes the physician liable for the penalty. In sum, then, where penalties are attached to the law, it is not unconceivable that those with wills will be needlessly underresuscitated and those without wills overresuscitated. [74]

In sumary, there is a very good chance that these new laws will collapse the spontaneous and healthy tension of medicine's "yes" to life and "no" to unauthorized manipulation. This tension is protected in the stipulation of "consent to treatment." Now it appears that the physician-patient covenant will be further eroded by invasive public policy. The adversary relations will replace the covenant and contractual relations. No doubt the present covenant is severely flawed. When "rapacious providers and ravenous consumers" (Illich) meet, the full furies of human sin are manifest. The answer is not more law. This only enforces and entices persons to deeper lawlessness. The answer is a fresh reinvigoration of the covenant of care.

We now turn to true pastoral experiences that seek to effect this very notion.

Meditation: *Karen Quinlan—The Search for a Time to Die*

Vex not his ghost: O, let him pass! He hates him
That would upon the rack of this tough world
Stretch him out longer.
>   *King Lear* (v. iii, 315-17)

"We know what she would say if she were here right now.
She'd say, 'It's time for me to go home now to my
Heavenly Father.' "
>   *Joseph Quinlan*

Q: Why am I born?
A: To know, love and serve God in this world and to be reunited with Him in the next.
>   *Ancient Catholic Catechism*

In every society the dominant image of death determines the prevalent concept of health! Our Western society is now struggling to clarify its understanding of death so that its sense of life might come into focus. We are not sure whether we are moving toward medical utopia or medical nemesis. We know that there is an obligation to die, but we are not sure that there is a right to die. We treasure health and vitality yet we know that we have vested it with too much meaning. As Kaspar Naegle has said, "Health flourishes best when least watched." Jesus said the same thing: "He who would save his life will lose it" (Matthew 16:25). Life in our day has become an irresistible idol, an overriding value. We treasure health and vitality. We do not experience life as Lear's plight, nor can we say with Sophocles in *Oedipus Colonneus*:

Never to have been born is best; and the next
best, by far, to return thence, by the way speediest,
where our beginnings are.

Though life still has the same transience that artists have always known, we do not experience it with the same tragic dimension. But although we cherish life and find it good, we also know, as Pascal has said, that it is deep moments, not duration, that signify.

June 21, 1977: The evening news tonight carries the report that Karen Quinlan has developed a serious infection. She will not be treated with antibiotics, this being seen as a heroic measure, say her doctors. Will she stabilize? Will she depart this place? Has her time come? "Karen still has some more work to do," says Elisabeth Kübler-Ross. "She is not yet ready to go." She lies today in her bed in New Jersey, a shriveled 60 pounds of her formerly robust 120, in fetal position her hands clasped as in prayer, tubes in her neck feeding her, catheters relieving her. She went to sleep one night and never woke up.

After considerable litigation, Judge Robert Muir, Jr., returned a forty page opinion, culminating the first stage of one of the most celebrated court cases in recent years. The opinion stated that the decision to terminate the life supports was a medical determination and in supporting this opinion it designated a court appointed guardian of the person of Miss Quinlan and also designated the step-father, Joseph Quinlan, the guardian of her property. The decision argued that it could only arbitrate on the temporal aspects of the case. This was a response to the religious argument that was presented by the family. Judge Muir determined "the most important temporal quality that she has is life." The court felt itself obliged to side in favor of this value. A final important theme in the opinion was the statement that there was not a constitutional right to die. A later court decision gave the parents the right to allow her to die, to withdraw life supports in consultation with their physicians. The respirator was disconnected. Karen continued to breathe.

Monumental spiritual and moral issues confront us in this case. The discussion of the lower court in this instance was not to make a decision. It contended that the law does not have domain in this realm of human experience. But as a symbolic case it captivates our attention. As individuals, in our families, as citizens and health professionals, we shall have to deal with this issue. What are the factors in our developing society that makes this a necessity? Sophisticated life-support technologies have ushered in a new era wherein we can no longer stand powerless before the onset of death. Many of the visitations of disease and debilitation that have previously ushered in our own death are now vulnerable to control. Sophisticated life-support technologies and the social phenomenon that Ivan Illich calls the medicalization of health come into play. These public values seek to draw more and more of the human experience at the threshold of death into the realm of advanced technology and well-equipped and highly complex health care institutions. These facts make it necessary for individuals, families, and health care professionals to face these decisions. The fact that we initiate life supports carries with it the correlative responsibility at one point of withdrawing those life supports. We cannot develop technological interventions and then disclaim continuing moral responsibility for their use.

The Quinlan case was the first legalized act of permitted, indirect, involuntary euthanasia in the United States. This effort to set a precedent in case law is paralleled by efforts within the legislative process. Here state lawmaking bodies are now being asked to make public policy determinations regarding the right to die and the obligation to preserve life.

Historical Aspects

At one time the physician was a priest. He was a mediator not only of physical and mental remedies but also the spiritual attendant at life's coming and going. Francis Bacon in the late 16th and early 17th centuries was both a physician and a clergyman. He was probably the first to catch a glimpse of the new era that was beginning to unfold wherein the task of the physician would be cast in more technological terms and his priestly function would be diminished. Bacon divided medicine into three offices: first, the preservation of health; second, the cure of disease; and third, prolongation of life. The last office, the prolongation of life, was a new function of medicine, bringing new knowledge and new therapeutic technique. And although it was, in Bacon's words, the most deficient, it was the most noble of the functions of medicine. This new sense of power and responsibility is difficult for us to accept, as is the tearing apart of the traditional unification of physician and pastor.

Reflecting the spirit of his age that life is short and brutish, Montaigne ridiculed the presumption that we should now transpose death more into the sphere of technique and deliberate decision.

> Tis the last and extreme form of dying. What an idle conceit it is to expect to die of a decay of strength which is the effect of the extremist age and to propose to ourselves no shorter lease on life. As if it were contrary to nature to see a man break his neck with a fall, be drowned by shipwreck, be snatched away with pleurosy or the plague. We ought to call natural death that which is general, common and universal.[75]

There is no constitutional right to die, wrote Judge Muir. What a strange response this is, living in a world of creatures that we know must die. The view is tantalizing and intriguing but, ultimately, futile. It reminds one of the phrase from Galen in his book *The Use of Limbs*. This ancient sage of medicine said: "It would be vain to expect to see living beings, formed of the blood of menstrous women and the semen of virile men, who will not die, will never feel pain or who will move perpetually, or who will shine like the sun." [76] Yet we are caught in a quest of imagination and creativity and we are not willing to accept the inevitability of death, let alone be its harbingers and facilitators. We see death as the offense, the enemy.

The Quinlan family left the court after Judge Muir's decision with heavy hearts. After the higher court judgment authorizing withdrawal of life supports there was relief, but also ambivalence. In the first case one felt relief that Judge Muir had made the decision that he had. They even talked of the courage that he expressed in the decision. There was a certain ambivalence in the family themselves as they asked for a judgment that the life supports be withdrawn. Yet the courage was undaunted. In our mood of medical mastery, we are like the ancient Germanic chieftains who raided the highly-civilized Roman Empire, destroyed the villages, raped the women and plundered all the goods—then would sit down and cry at what they had done. The medical feat is a pyrrhic victory. A mood of remorse followed the Germanic expression of power and control. So in the case of Karen Quinlan. Had Judge Muir determined that the life supports should be withdrawn, had he directed the family or physician to "pull the plug," there would have also been a remorse, a resentment that this had to be done. This indeed became the case in the later decision. So we are in the realm of a truly ethical decision. This is a realm where moral certainty is completely lacking, and where one must make a risk-fraught decision with the knowledge that he will not be completely right or completely wrong, but that he must bear the consequences for the decisions he has made. Only a vivid biblical sense of grace and forgiveness could sustain one in this moral morass.

Spiritual Aspects

The theological argument of the Quinlan family is an intriguing facet of the case. The impassioned reasoning sounded to our skeptical ears like an ancient voice from some bygone age of faith. Karen's life, they argued, had already ceased in every sense except the physical and mechanical. She was unconscious, her mind was irreversibly damaged, she had no capacity for relation. She was in a vegetative state. We should allow her to collapse into the natural state where her body, unassisted by life-supports, would quickly exhaust the remaining measure of vitality. God has come to receive her life and we should allow her to die. Mr. Quinlan, a devout Roman Catholic, expressed his views in this kind of theological language. "Let us allow Karen to return to her natural state so that we can place her body in the tender loving hands of the Lord." It is the Lord's will that she be allowed to die." "Take from her the machines and the tubes connected to her. Let her pass into the hands of the Lord."

Judge Muir pondered this argument with great deliberation. His response was not to deny the validity of the Quinlan arguments, but to delimit the area of the court's responsibility. He said in his decision, "the most important temporal quality that she has is life." In other words the court can only make determinations regarding temporal and material qualities. It cannot adjudicate in the other areas of human existence. He seemed to be echoing a sentiment that was expressed vividly by Pearl Buck when commenting on the question of abortion. "When all we know of what lies beyond this life is surmise, it is not safe or prudent to wager against life."

What lies beyond this place? This becomes the key spiritual issue of the case. If this life is all there is, perhaps we should cling tenaciously to any fragment of existence, even vegetation. But there is another view which holds that this life is but the prelude to that fuller expression of life, which lies beyond our death. Certain elements in this view explain at least one of the reasons why religion is seen to be a continuing enemy of medicine. In the Morristown courtroom the priests and the family were on one side of the debate, the neurologists and neurosurgeons and attorneys on the other side.

Occasionally the physicians with whom I have worked will comment on the deep motivational factors that provide impulse for their experimental and clinical work. Death is seen as an offense and a contradiction. It is not a part of nature; it is an intrusion into what nature should be. The destructive power of the forces of death, disease, and debilitation should eventually be overcome. To accept death or to will your own death is a sin, a crime, and a sickness in our society. This is part of the modern mentality wherein death is seen as an obscenity, as something to be masqueraded, camouflaged, and cosmetized.

Yet the persuasion that death is natural and good is also wanting. Gross injustices and inhumanities have been perpetrated on other individuals down through the ages in the name of God and in the service of the eternal life that lies beyond this physical life. The conquistadors in Latin America baptized children and then rushed them into eternity. The downtrodden have often been urged to endure injustice now because of the heavenly bliss that follows. There is a perennial tendency in the human spirit to demean and cheapen life and see it as expendable in ourselves and, more often, in others. There is a lingering mood in our culture that is described by Norman Mailer as "a middle class lust for destruction."

Yet a mature physician will find strength and beauty in the person who is ready to die when death's inevitability is apparent. Peace in the face of death is the mark of deep faith and trust. Jesus spoke, probably to those facing martyrdom, "In my Father's house are many rooms. I go to prepare a place for you. . . . I will come again and will take you to myself" (John 14:2-4).

In a very interesting way, the law has come to grips with this theme of taking your own life. In British common law, for example, suicide came to be seen as a form of homicide. The history is most intriguing. In medieval Britain there was a law that said that property and goods could be taken from the wealthy if they were accused of treason. Because of this statute, many wealthy noblemen were accused surreptitiously of treason so that their lands could be confiscated and the king could be enriched. Responding to this many noblemen would commit suicide so that they would die before their lands could be confiscated. Then the law we have stated came into being, where the act of suicide was seen as a crime and goods and properties were thus confiscated. The person who committed suicide was buried at the crossroads with an iron stake driven through his heart. Blackstone, in his commentary on the British law, wrote:

> Self murder is the pretended heroism but real cowardice of the Stoic philosophers who destroyed themselves to avoid those ills which they had not the fortitude to endure. The law of England

wisely and religiously concurs that no man hath a power to destroy life but by commission from God, the author of it, and as their suicide is guilty of a double offence, one spiritual, in evading the prerogative of the Almighty and rushing into his immediate presence uncalled for, the other temporal against the King, who has an interest in the preservation of all his subjects.[77]

In the spirit of this ancient legal tradition, Judge Muir determined that the court could not make a decision on the basis of these arguments. The court only had interest and domain in the material and temporal realm of human existence. But this separation of reality does not really help. We are realizing more and more the connection between the spiritual and the temporal world. Man is developing intellectual powers and technologies to increase his controls over the thresholds of birth and death and he must now use these knowledgeably and responsibly. To use theological language, we can say that God is giving these realms of knowledge to us and we will be held responsible for their proper use.

The Judeo-Christian God is the author and finisher of life. People of the Sinai and Golgotha covenants are commanded to love the neighbor, to honor the weak and helpless, to protect and enhance life. The taking of life in suicide, homicide, or genocide is contrary to divine, natural, and positive law. Life is given to persons for a possibility hidden in the divine purpose. To rise up and in malice destroy another is an attack on God himself.

Yet our life is not an end in itself. We are not obliged to de-destroy life in the name of preserving it. Christian moralists, including those who have spoken at the Quinlan case, have testified that there is no moral duty to sustain by extraordinary means the vital functions of the body. If the interventions only prolong the suffering and increase the injury, there is no moral constraint to continue.

On the other hand, the presence of suffering in the patient and the agony of the death watch in the family is not seen as absurd and meaningless in this religious frame. Relief of pain is not the "end all" value of spiritual existence. This is rather a novel, hedonistic value that symbolizes the superficiality of our culture. When suffering comes it has the capacity to be God's megaphone (C. S. Lewis), asking who we are, what we are becoming, and whose we are.

In the midst of his pain, the psalmist cried:

> Nevertheless I am continually
>   with thee;
>   thou dost hold my right hand.
> Thou dost guide me with thy
>   counsel,
>   and afterward thou wilt receive
>   me to glory.
> Whom have I in heaven but thee?
>   And there is nothing upon
>   earth that I desire besides
>   thee.
> My flesh and my heart may fail,
>   but God is the strength of my
>   heart and my portion forever.
>   *Psalm* 73:23-26

On Dying Well

In 1974, the General Synod Board for Social Responsibility of the Church of England issued a provocative and insightful report entitled *On Dying Well*.[78] The report attempts to refresh the classic meanings of the concept of euthanasia while stripping the word of its pejorative connotations. The four-year study—initiated under the chairmanship of the brilliant theologian Ian Ramsey, Bishop of Durham—profited by the incisive philosophical insight of R. M. Hare and the clinical wisdom of Dr. Cicely Saunders of St. Christopher's Hospice in London.

The report is based on the premise that only religion can remind us that the pilgrimage of persons involves living and dying. "The individual is conceived to enjoy, in some sense, a right to die" (p. 6). Death is part of the pattern of life. It is an essential form and color in the portrait of existence. Death must be acknowledged, accepted and responded to in responsible stewardship. While the impulses of denial, optimism, and downright disgust in the face of death are very human, they need to be transformed by the nobler impulses of the human spirit—candor, courage and humility—so that death can be anticipated, confronted and conquered with the full natural powers and extrinsic graces that enliven man.

The report is careful to differentiate among different types of initiatives in hastening death. It is not concerned to justify mercy killing, nor is it interested in rationalizing suicide. It is concerned with *dying well* in the context of human care and scientific knowledge. Several elements are highlighted to help people die well.

First, it is acknowledged that at times there exists an unavoidable tension between the mandates to alleviate suffering and to prolong life. Indeed efforts in pursuit of the former often contradict the latter. In cases where therapeutic and curative measures are no longer meaningful, medical care takes on a new function: to care and comfort. "The appropriate treatment is therefore good nursing care and use of pain killing drugs where necessary. It is wrong to think that medicine has now no more to do; it has a function that requires skills, care and attention of a high order" (p. 9).

The second major point in the Commission's analysis is a recognition of the moral complexity of medical situations where taking life seems to be the lesser of two evils. It may indeed be the case, as in the situation where a truck driver is pinned, cannot be rescued, and will soon burn to death in a slow excruciating way, that it is morally justifiable to introduce another mortal force, in this case, a gunshot.

It must be acknowledged that in the modern world, in sophisticated teaching hospitals, the moral dynamics are extremely complex, precisely because the technical powers are so advanced. To diminish death in one area means to increase it in another.

Withholding the mortal force of a malignant tumor through chemo and radiation therapy is to knowingly increase the danger of massive infection because of the immuno-suppression of the initial treatment. In a very real sense then, medical doctors knowingly intensify morbid and mortal forces in their therapeutic administrations.

In a similar way, as the chances for thorough treatment vanish, doctors lessen the interventions. In short, accumulating knowledge and interventive power forces moral confrontations and decisive action. It is morally scandalous to be medically aggressive at one point and then feign passivity and unwillingness to follow through on a course of action at another.

The final policy recommendation is that voluntary euthanasia not be legalized; that it continue to be proscribed. While in extreme cases it will be seen as morally licit, it would be wrong and dangerous to alter the law. "The law is a blunt instrument for dealing with moral complexities and it is better to allow hard cases to be taken care of by the various expedients that are available than to introduce a new principle which would turn out to be too permissive" (p. 12).

The section on theological analysis attempts to ground a moral position on initiatives in dying on the doctrine of God as creator and redeemer. Citing the inconclusivity of both natural law and Scripture, the report argues that "respect for God's creation requires us to refrain from any unnecessary destruction of it" (p. 17). When, therefore, "there are other measures available of exercising care and compassion towards a person in his dying and of relieving his ultimate distress, respect for God's creation and for the consequent value of human life in general would tell against the practice of euthanasia" (p. 18).

But death is an event in the divine destiny of human life. "Death has a Godward dimension as well as manward and natural dimensions" (p. 19). Death is that moment of rendezvous, of confrontation with the "last enemy." It is a grand moment when faith is verified; it is the occasion when one "is finally to prove the love and power of God in Christ" (p. 19). According to this concept, suicide or hastened death is cowardly and an expression of lack of trust in God.

Death is also an interactional event. Man's life-setting includes family, neighbors, and limited resources. To categorically prohibit or permit euthanasia would be a breach of moral wisdom. This section concludes: "The good and simple principle that innocent human life is sacred has influenced profoundly our conviction that the old and the dying should be cared for and consoled, no matter what their condition" (p. 24).

While the report offers strong proscriptions regarding how persons ought not to die, the positive statement of how one can die well is lacking. The middle and end sections written by Dr. Saunders move cautiously in this direction. People can die well. They can be eased toward their death by thoughtful pain killing medication and attentive care. Decisive at this point are attitudes, mood, and milieu. The report stops short of elaboration at this critical point. It remains for us, then, to do some serious theological work which can form the basis for faithful and artful dying and care for the dying. To this task we must now move.

We have briefly described the struggles of our society to find and define something that could be called natural death. For personal and political reasons it is imperative that we press on to stipulate what we mean by *natural* and *timely* death. Daniel Callahan offers an insightful definition containing the requisite elements.

> Natural death is the individual event of death at that point in a life when (a) one's life work has been accomplished, (b) one's moral obligations to those for whom one has had responsibility have been discharged, (c) one's death will not seem to others an offense to sense or sensibility, or tempt others to despair and rage at human existence, and finally (d) one's process of dying is not marked by unbearable and degrading pain.[79]

While operative definitions may be possible, the search for a universal sense will elude us. It is a necessary but futile quest because it will never be satisfactorily resolved. But that is good. The causes of death should remain as challenges that we strive to understand and counter. Death itself will remain as the bittersweet conclusion of the struggle. As man goes toward death, the mingled rage and resignation will remain the perpetual marks of his indomitable glory.

V

The Theology
of Human Death

Who knows that death is not life
and life not death?
Euripides

THE PARADOX OF SORROW in the midst of joy, of death in the midst of life makes man a religious being. Death makes theology irresistible. Conversely, it is the nature of man as revealed by our knowledge of God that contains the tension between flesh and spirit, finitude and eternal life. The being of God sets in motion the tension in man's being. The doctrine of man as a creature created in God's image teaches that man must always be restless in both the creatureliness and godliness of his life. A human being is "a little lower than God, yet ruler over all He has made, crowned with glory and honor" (Psalm 8).

If it is theology that discloses man's life as contradictory and paradoxical, it is also theology that can clarify both the nature and purpose of the paradox. The meaning of things can be disclosed as we discover the being who means it. In this chapter we will first examine the various strains of theology of death that operate in Western culture. Then we will look at the bibli-

101

cal understanding of death climaxing in the meaning of the
death of Christ. Finally we will single out the key motifs that
contribute to our understanding of human initiatives in dying.

Two Approaches to Death

Two quite distinct understandings of death are found in our
culture. One approach stresses death as friend—this is the Greek
strain. The other accents death as enemy and has Hebraic
roots. In one tradition death is natural. In the other it is unnatural. John Hick, in his masterful study, *Death and Eternal
Life*,[80] finds two fundamentally different types of theology at
the root of these two variant cultural images. Both are found
in the earliest expressions of Christian piety. One strain, influenced perhaps by the Greeks and Stoics, talks of "going toward
God" in death. Death is the event where the loving Lord of our
life receives back that life that he loaned us in the first place. We
go to "live with Christ" and fully experience what we have fore-
tasted under the conditions of existence as eternal life.

The other strain is Judaic. It is introduced into Christian
thought and life by the Apostle Paul. Death is punishment for
sin. "As sin came into the world through one man (Adam)
and death through sin so death spread to all men because all
had sinned" (Romans 5:12).

This view became dominant in the Christian world through
Augustine in the fifth century.

> It is above all Augustine . . . who first wove the dark themes
> of guilt, remorse and punishment into the tremendous drama
> of creation, heaven and hell which has dominated the Christian
> imagination in the West until the last hundred years or so.[81]

In the eleventh century, Anselm wrote a work which signifi-
cantly shaped Western culture. In *Cur Deus Homo?* he wrote:

> That also (man) was created as that he was not under the
> necessity of dying, may hence be easily proved, since, as we
> said before, it is contrary to the wisdom and justice of God that

He should compel man, whom He made upright for everlasting happiness, to suffer death for no fault. It follows, therefore, that had man never sinned, he never would have died.[82]

Here we locate a formative element which shapes the death understanding of people in Western Christian culture. It is Christian thought, under the impact of Paul, Augustine, and Anselm, that has fashioned a culture which sees death as an evil intrusion into the supposed order of things. This notion above all prompts our philosophy of science and our technological venture against disease. This theology of death holds that death and its causes—disease, war, accidents—are diabolic forces introduced into creation with the fall. They are marks in the creation which sting and offend. They are aberrations in nature. They are to be endured as forces that once were not and that one day will not be. Man responds with the full fury of his resistance and reason.

This is not to say that there is only resistance against death in Western culture and only submission in Hellenic and Eastern civilization. The two-fold dynamic is also present everywhere and at all times. But the Pauline view remains dominant in the West through the Renaissance and Reformation and forward to the Enlightenment. Let us look at both concepts.

The Greek Theology of Death

In his important study, *Death and Neurosis*, J. E. Meyer claims that:

> The attitude of Christianity to dying and death results historically from three diverse and in part contrasting traditions: the severe inner-worldliness of the Jewish Yahweh faith, the Greek dualism of the immortal soul, and the belief in resurrection as found in the New Testament. In the Old Testament, birth and death are strict boundaries enclosing life. Death is an evil ordained by divine judgment, but it is also the definitive ending of a life fulfilled. The doctrine of the immortality of the soul, with which the Greek world from Homer to Hellenism is imbued, continued to exert its influence by way of the Christian church and finally came into prominence again in a modified form in the Age of Enlightenment and in German idealism.[83]

Greek thought about death evolves through several stages and continues to endure as a richly nuanced tradition in the modern world. The Renaissance and Enlightenment together with some forms of modern humanistic thought stand directly in the tradition. The earliest Greeks saw death in terms of its awful and tragic necessity. Homer has Achilles say:

> Speak not smoothly of death, I beseech you, O famous Odysseus. Better by far to remain on earth in the thrall of another . . . rather than reign sole king in the realm of bodyless phantoms.[84]

Over against the sad and foreboding "realm of bodyless phantoms," the heroic assertion of life was the only appropriate response. Glorious deeds in battle, high civic responsibility, and human courage are the only ways that mortals snatch some measure of immortality from the gods.

Quite different from the spirit of Homer is another view of death illustrated by Pythagoras (572-497 B.C.). He thought that the soul was separable from the body, and that it would finally be reunited with the Divine. This soul/body tension with its emphasis on the passage and purification of the soul is an ancient strain derived from primitive orphic cults and Dionysian rites. It shapes the thought of Plato, Aristotle, the Hippocratic medical tradition and early Christian thought. Although the Renaissance and Enlightenment abandon some of the religious qualities, the same structural view of man (soul/body) is retained.

In Plato we find the sublime heights of the Greek philosophy of death. Socrates, in the *Apology,* affirms:

> . . . I do believe that there are gods, and in a sense higher than that in which any of my accusers believed in them. And since there is God, no evil can happen to a good man, neither in life or after death.[85]

For Socrates, the existence of God insures the moral quality of the universe and even death must have a purpose.

The Greek view of death, like the Greek view of soul and body, continues to infiltrate Christian thought. In Plotinus (A.D. 204-270), the last great thinker of antiquity, the Platonic dualism, with its emphasis on soul-life and ecstasy, is fully drawn.

> Many times this happened: lifted out of the body in to myself; becoming external to all other things and self-centered; beholding a marvelous beauty, then more than ever, assured of community with loftiest order. . . .[86]

Plotinus could easily provide descriptions of near-death and post-death experience for Elisabeth Kübler-Ross or Raymond Moody. The narratives are similar to those these physicians have recorded.

Indeed the romantic mood is capitulated down through the centuries in Western civilization. Greek revival occurs perennially in our culture. Schelling (1775-1854) and German idealism provided spiritual undergirding to the Enlightenment. "How wonderful is death," Schelling writes, speaking of the death of Keats.

> He is made one with Nature; there is heard
> His voice in all her music, from the moan
> Of thunder to the song of night's sweet bird.
>
> *Adonis* [87]

The Greek view of the attractiveness of death is popularized in the little book of Dr. Raymond A. Moody, Jr., *Life After Life*.[88] As he relates the experience of dying in some patients, he describes the irresistible drawing of a "Being of light." At death's door, this Being interrogates us in a totally loving and accepting way. The moment of reckoning and accounting has neither approval nor condemnation to it. It merely recounts all the events of one's life, both those things that one remembers with gratitude and those events one wishes to forget. In a recent address, Elisabeth Kübler-Ross reflected on the after-life of Adolf Hitler from this same romantic Greek persuasion. Far from Dante's perpetual punishment in hell, this despicable creature is slowly led to insight and restoration. She goes so far as to say that without Hitler, she would not be involved in her work on dying. (Shortly after the war, she visited the concentration camps in Czechoslovakia and Poland.) Hitler must recount over and over the misdeeds that marked his life until slowly he is drawn to the truth of things. Here Kübler-Ross and Moody are attempting to revive the convictions of the Greek immortalists who, believing in universal salvation, thought that the soul must be purged and cleansed so that it might become akin to the purity of the Divine Soul.

Moody is offended by the Hebrew notion of judgment. He bends over backward to say that the experiences of accounting of life events reported to him are not to be misconstrued as evidence of the classic Christian notions of judgment, heaven and hell.

> Through all of my research, however, I have not heard a single reference to a heaven or hell or anything like the customary picture to which we are exposed in this society.[89]

The questions that must be raised of Moody's research are: How extensive is the clinical experience? What thought forms, beliefs, religious notions, and repressions does the doctor bring to the interaction with the patient? What is the meaning of "life after life" in our culture? Is it the kind of heaven and hell portrayed by Bible Belt fundamentalism? Moody must know that these ingredients, Hebrew and Greek, interplay in our culture and in our personal consciousness, coloring the ways we experience events and interpret their meaning.

The Hebraic Theology of Death

The three great Abrahamic traditions—Judaism, Christianity and Islam—all accept a view of life and death based on the ancient story of Adam and Eve. A primordial human transgression has invited death into the creation.

Before exploring this position in detail, it must be noted that a divergent strain also appears in Judaism and the Koran. The Wisdom literature of the ancient Near East, which finds classic expression in the Book of Ecclesiastes, holds that death is a natural, necessary and good part of the creation.

The importance of noting this divergent tradition is to illustrate our thesis that the paradox is perpetual and is never completely resolved. Within a tradition where the view of death as enemy is dominant and normative, the view of death as friend persists. The biblical tradition portrays a development as it seeks to grapple with the meaning of death. As the unfolding of divine revelation, it discloses to us how we ought to live in the face of death and how we are to die. In the Old and New Testaments we find the accumulation of insight through the adding of successive layers or dimensions. Each new level sharpens the picture. Together they constitute a full disclosure of spiritual and moral wisdom about death.

At the base level is the fundamental fact that we are creatures who, like the plants and other animals, will be cut down in due time. Like stalks, we will be harvested when ripe (Job 5:26). Like the grass and flower, we will wither, fade, dry up, and blow away (Isaiah 40:6). The life span is a divine gift (Genesis 6:3; Psalm 90:10). It runs its course and passes away. Having written our chapter, the story of life goes on. What follows death is relatively unimportant. The images are shadowy. The dead may continue to exist in Sheol, but that is a stale, ephemeral, and non-vital existence. It is uninteresting.

But even this rudimentary level of insight reveals what death means. It addresses the question of why death exists. To the Hebrew, God gives death. He withdraws his Spirit, and life collapses back to its constituent elements. The life course and our awareness of its brevity is given for a purpose. We are to number our days, to seek wisdom (Psalm 90:12). Death, even at this basic level, is both curse and gift. It is the searing wrath of God that moves relentlessly through his creation, consummating his purpose, effecting his justice and mercy. Dying and the premonitions of mortality are the divine invitation to the secret place where we come to know what life is all about.

A later level of interpretation presents death as a tearing apart of body and soul, an exhaustion from the body of the Spirit of Life (Genesis 35:18; 1 Kings 17:21; Jeremiah 15:9; Jonah 4:3). Life is a gift from God which he receives back at death. Here again we gain instruction that our life is precarious and tentative, held in vital balance by God's active will. G. K. Chesterton has remarked that all vitality and movement is a miracle. It is only our facile presumption that leads us to expect the sun, of necessity, to rise each day and one breath to follow another. Better to *trust* that these regularities will occur because the Being who means and sustains the creation says: "do it again!"

At yet another level of biblical insight, death begins to take on a moral dimension. Surely man dies like a beast and with natural inevitability. Yet his death comes as a sting. Because of his propensity for evil, man dies; and the fact that he is death-bound intensifies the evil in his life. Death is the end of the path of disobedience (Deuteronomy 30:19). Illness, war and other calamities are also consequences of sin. Healing is deliverance from death (Psalm 9:13; Luke 15:24). These themes accent the redemptive and salvific qualities of suffering and death. Alienation from God and rebellion lead only to strife and death. The theme of sacrificial death becomes acute. The scapegoat, the lamb of God, the servant—must die to atone for the wrong of the people.

Perhaps it seems that only a cruel, harsh, deity would exact such a price for sin. But it is more realistic and understandable when we think of actual human transactions. As one observes and participates in interactions with other people, it becomes clear how enmity builds up and intensifies. Cruelty and violence seem to be inevitable and irresistible. Finally crisis erupts and only great suffering and/or death can cleanse and restore life and community.

West Side Story is an excellent modern adaptation of the ancient Romeo and Juliet story. Here we have feuding factions, gangs who tear at each other's throats. The hatred goes deep. It is personal and ethnic. It concerns turf and pride and survival. Then Tony and Maria meet—an Italian and a Pole—and love reaches across the barrier. Evil and misunderstanding increase, but so does love. Events climax in a street fight and death. Finally through suffering and death, reconciliation occurs. This is the essence of the biblical witness, and of the Christ message. It tells us about what we see before our very eyes all the time.

The Death of Christ

At the heart of the Christian gospel is the affirmation that the cross of Jesus Christ is not only the meaning of life but also the answer to death. Jesus' death is accessible to the historian. He was crucified under Pontius Pilate. His death is noted by non-Christians (Tacitus *Annals*, XV. 44, Josephus *Antiquities*, XVIII, iii 3). On the surface, he died for political crimes (Luke 23:2; Mark 15:26; John 19:19ff). The Gospel writers and Paul show the deeper significance. Jesus accepted his death intentionally. Dying was at the center of his vocation. Ever since his baptism it was made clear that the Son of Man would suffer (Mark 1:11; 8:31; Luke 24:31). He consciously identified himself as the suffering servant on whom is laid the chastisement of our peace (Isaiah 52, 53).

It is the grand drama of humiliation and exaltation, suffering and restoration, death and resurrection that portrays the meaning of life and death in Christian theology. For Jesus, death is an adversary that must be struggled with (Mark 14:32; Hebrews 5:7). Although the Pauline emphasis on death as the "last enemy" (1 Corinthians 15:26) is not explicit in Jesus' teaching about death in the Gospels, the sense is there. As he dies, Jesus cries: "It is finished!" (John 19:30).

The life of humility, dying to self, patient courage and sacrificial love is commended to believers in early Christian preaching. We are to "take up our cross" (Matthew 16:24), "die every day" (1 Corinthians 15:31), and "die unto the Lord" (Romans 14:8). "To die is gain" (Philippians 1:21), a phrase commonly found in the Greeks, is invested with new meaning. When Sophocles has Antigone says: "Such (premature) death is gain. Yes, surely gain . . ." he is talking of release from the torment of life, "to one so overwhelmed with trouble." [90] Death is gain for the Christian because life is Christ. A new quality of existence is introduced which death does not have power to interrupt. The Christian Gospel argues that life is discovered in death, that self-awareness and vitality are bestowed as one dies to self, that in the foolishness of the cross is contained all the wisdom of God (1 Corinthians 1:24). One goes toward death, therefore, with both trepidation and anticipation.

Teilhard de Chardin prays:

> At that moment when I feel I am losing hold of myself and am absolutely passive within the hands of the great unknown forces that have formed me . . . O God, grant that I may understand that it is You (provided only my faith is strong enough) who are painfully parting the fibres of my being in order to penetrate to the very marrow of my substance and bear me away within Yourself." [91]

In summary, the theology that forms Western culture both celebrates life, (abhorring death), and at the same time divests life of ultimate importance, (welcoming death). The theological roots of our culture will therefore sustain a flourishing of science and technology but also criticize it.

It will nurture and support the medical profession but will always remain suspicious of it. Cultures influenced by Christian thought and devotion will never honor or condone suicide, yet they will nurture in their sons and daughters a strange fascination and yearning for death.

To be healthy in body, mind, and soul is to live with the paradox of death in the midst of life. In the chapter on paradoxes in the great study of *Orthodoxy*, Chesterton summarized:

A man cut off by the sea may save his life if he will risk it on the precipice. He can only get away from death by continually stepping within an inch of it. A soldier surrounded by enemies, if he is to cut his way out, needs to combine a strong desire for living with a strange carelessness about dying. He must not merely cling to life, for then he will be a coward, and he will not escape. He must not merely wait for death, for then he will be a suicide, and will not escape. He must seek his life in a spirit of furious indifference to it; he must desire life like water and yet drink death like wine. No philosopher, I fancy has ever expressed this romantic riddle with adequate lucidity, and I certainly have not done so. But Christianity has done more: it has marked the limits of it in the awful graves of the suicide and the hero, showing the distance between him who dies for the sake of living and him who dies for the sake of dying. And it has held up ever since above the European lances the banner of the mystery of chivalry: the Christian courage, which is a disdain of death; not the Chinese courage, which is a disdain of life.[92]

VI

Immortality
and Life after Life

Beware of the man whose God is in the sky.
> G. B. *Shaw*

Talk to me about the truth of religion and I'll listen gladly,
Talk to me about the duty of religion and I'll listen submissively.
But don't come talking to me about the consolations of religion
or I shall suspect that you don't understand.[93]
> C. S. *Lewis*

FASCINATION WITH LIFE AFTER LIFE becomes more prevalent
in times when people have grown weary with the tasks of
building a better world here and now. Today everyone
you meet in the hospital has tales of life after life, of messages
back from the dead. Social commentators call it a day of the
blueing or cooling of America. The age of critical protest at
social conditions—war, racism, sexism, nuclear proliferation—has
waned and a new generation has appeared, searching for security, satisfactions, and success.

The spiritual root of this condition is to be found in a defective
theology. The tension of the life/death equation has collapsed.
Disdain for life has given way to a yearning for death and that

113

which lies beyond death. The suicide rate of young adolescents has recently increased. A common denominator in these cases is the supposed attraction of "that other world" in contrast to the burdens of this. Dr. Bill Bartholome, a pediatrician at our Medical Center, finds the element of religiosity frequently present in youthful suicide attempts. Our relation to death is determined by the influence or absence of religious ideas about the beyond. In this chapter we will (1) explore the evolution of the idea of immortality; (2) review and critique the contemporary interest in life after life and (3) note the political and medical quest for an indefinite extension of life. The chapter will close with a reflection on anabiosis (returning to life) and immortality.

The Idea of Immortality

Man has always been a contradictory being as he lives in the face of death. Alone among the animals, he knows that he will die. Yet he tries to deny it. When Elvis Presley collapsed and died a 42-year-old nurse—and millions of other people—were shocked. The death of Elvis was a cruel reminder that persons her age and younger do, indeed, die. In our hoping and our anticipating, there is something that fosters the illusion that as much lies before us as lies behind.

As soon as man appeared on the earth he undertook a ritual practiced by no other species. He prepared burial places for his own kind. Even if exigencies of life require mass graves, or tombs of unknown soldiers, or if (as in the caste of the POWs and MIAs from the Vietnam war) the remains cannot be located, some human gesture of remembrance and provision for immortality seems necessary. Not only does man respectfully lay his friends to rest, his burial customs betray unmistakably that he believes that life continues after one expires. Peking Man, Neanderthal Man, and the Cro-Magnons who roamed the lands that would become Europe and Eurasia—each put away foods, artifacts, tools, weapons, and even wives, to accompany the deceased into the beyond.

Now this custom does not prove life after life, nor does it prove the existence of God. All it proves is the hope in some beyond, and the sense of absurdity that this little light should be allowed to flame brightly, then flicker and die.

The earliest beliefs in immortality focused on the restless soul wandering in some abode of the dead.

Lucien Levy-Brühl has examined the lives of savage peoples in Australia and conjectured that the primitive notion of immortality is accompanied by the belief that death is an enemy. There is a general assumption that persons should not die. Some trick must have been pulled, some hex placed on the victim. People did not die; they were killed.[94] Though the departed are severed from contact with home and friends, they wish to remain in contact, they continue to exert influence, they expect honor and fear. It must be remembered that prehistoric man's life-span averaged 18 years and he usually died violently.[95]

Death was not an inviting event, nor was immortality something one anticipated. It remained for the emergence of the great religions to make life beyond life a desirable thing. According to the religious mind, human life has value and the universe is moral and benevolent. In ancient Egypt and Greece, and in the Semitic traditions and other great eighth century B.C. religious movements, the goodness of the Creator is seen to imply the provision of blessedness for the faithful when they die. In the *Odyssey*, for example, the sea god tells King Menelaus that

> the deathless gods will convey thee to the Elysian plain and the world's end, where is Rhodamanthus of the fair hair, where life is easiest for men. No snow is there, nor yet any great storm, nor any rain; but always the ocean sendeth forth the breeze of the shrill West to blow cool on men. Yea, for thou hast Helen to wife, and thereby they deem thee to be a son of Zeus.[96]

Great Hebrew heroes Elijah and Enoch (2 Kings 2:11; Genesis 5:24) were transported to heaven without death. Death was the purifying fire that their righteous lives did not require.

At first, only certain people—great kings or spiritual leaders—
were considered to be immortal. They represented the masses in
the life to come. In Greece, these were descendants or the favor-
ites of the gods. In Israel, they were the servants of God. In
some cultures there was an entire class of immortals.

Slowly persons came to be seen as unique individuals. Discreet
and valuable in and of themselves, they became the bearers of
immortality. One of the earliest references to this concept is an
inscription on the tomb of a nobleman called Herkhuf (ca. 2300
B.C. which claims

> I gave bread to the hungry, clothing to the naked, I ferried
> him who had no boat. . . . Never did I say aught evil. . . . I
> desired that it might be well with me in the Great God's pres-
> ence.[97]

We see now the beginnings of the tendency to place immortality in a moral context. In the Egyptian *Book of the Dead* (ca.
2000 B.C.) we have the image of the god Osiris, before whom
people are called to account for their lives. Man's heart is
weighed against a feather which represents righteousness. Osiris
sits on the judgment seat reviewing the plaintiffs who request
immortality because they have not robbed, lied, defiled a man's
wife, or cursed the king. They base their claim for immortality
on their adherence to the law.[98]

In Judaism a refinement of the theological sense of death and
immortality occurs in the eighth and seventh century prophets.
Jeremiah reflects the notion of corporate guilt or immortality:
"Every one shall die for his own sin; each man who eats sour
grapes, his teeth shall be set on edge" (Jeremiah 31:30). Ezekiel
places death and afterlife purely in the moral and relational
context of one's life before God. "Behold all souls are mine; the
soul of the father as well as the soul of the son is mine: the soul
that sins shall die" (Ezekiel 18:4).

At this point it is necessary to the development of our thesis
to understand the doctrine of body and soul that develops in
prophetic Judaism. As we noted earlier, the Greeks believed

that man was an immortal soul living for awhile in a mortal body. Images like prison and release, cocoon and butterfly were used to describe the departure of soul from body in death. The Hebrews did not believe that the body housed a soul. They believed that the soul contained the body. In Wheeler Robinson's phrase, man is an "animated body, not an incarnated soul." [99] The German philosopher, Max Scheler argues that just as during life the personality cannot be contained by the physical body, so in death the spiritual body will not come to and end when the physical body has deteriorated.[100]

Modern Western culture has many rich and intense views on life after life. One widely-held position is that this life is all there is, and one should not waste time in conjecture about what lies beyond.

Western Christian civilization generally holds a view of life beyond life that is colored by Greek and Hebraic elements. The Greek body-soul dualism and the notion of the soul's natural immortality live on strongly in the beliefs of people today. Likewise the Hebrew sense of moral requirement in life, and of death as judgment and conquest is deeply formative. The Hebrew strain is mediated through Christianity with the strong notes of atonement, reconciliation and victory over death through the vicarious incorporation into him who is the second Adam. By the first Adam came death into the world, by the second came resurrection and life (1 Corinthians 15:22).

In the one tradition immortality is a natural endowment. In the other tradition eternal life is an act of God, a gift. Cullman writes:

> Only he who apprehends with the first Christians the horror of death, who takes death seriously as death, can comprehend the Easter exultation of the primitive Christian community and understand that the whole thinking of the New Testament is governed by the belief in the Resurrection. Belief in the immortality of the soul is not belief in a revolutionary event. Immortality, in fact, is only a *negative* assertion: the soul does *not* die, but simply lives on. Resurrection is a *positive* assertion: the whole man, who has really died, is recalled to life by a new

act of creation by God. Something has happened—a miracle of
creation! For something has also happened previously, something fearful: life formed by God has been destroyed.[101]

Life After Life

When we see the spiritual roots of our culture that have
shaped our thought regarding death and immortality, it is not
surprising to find recurrence of periods of intense fascination
with life after life. We live today in such a period. The Bridey
Murphy phenomenon, Bishop Pike communicating back from
the other side, and now the reporting of post-death stages by
physicians Elisabeth Kübler-Ross and Raymond Moody all suggest to us that we are moving into a new era where immortality will increasingly become the focus of human concentration.

Authors have suggested various reasons for this new consciousness. Paul Goodman [102] and Hans Morgenthau [103] have suggested
that people today fear annihilation via nuclear holocaust or environmental crisis. This fear forces our minds to construct images
of immortality. I believe that this preoccupation with immortality arises from our living at the end of an era of tremendous
confidence in science and technology, a confidence that has not
been fulfilled. As man moved into the beginning of this century
he was confident that great power, technology and wealth would
usher in bliss heretofore unknown. We thought that medicine
would conquer disease. We thought that war would cease as national leaders became more rational and communications im-
proved.

Instead we have seen technology unleash the greatest devastation yet to occur in human history. The factories, machines, and
computers have depersonalized lives as much as they have presented new opportunities. Wealth has not brought happiness.

Medicine, far from ushering in an era of disease-free existence,
has actually contributed to the formation of "the sick society."
Measured any way—morbidity, hospital time, or cost—we are
sicker at the end of the age of biomedical progress than we were
when it started. We turn in dissatisfaction from the frustrated

efforts of our ingenuity, our justice and our compassion and seek anchors outside of this life. Failing to find peace on earth, we seek inner peace. Failing to sense power and confidence in the tasks of life, we seek the escape comforts of drugs, entertainments, and the like. Failing to sense the moral imperatives to get to work and renew this world which is our heritage and trust, we yearn to be transported beyond this world and this life.

The book *Life After Life* by Dr. Raymond Moody illustrates a coming to grips with the uncertainty of death. "Actual case histories that reveal there is life after death," reads the headline on the cover.[104] Extrapolating from a small number of cases, Moody suggests a series of stages that constitute the experience of dying. These include in sequence: Ineffability, Hearing the News, Feelings of Peace and Quiet, the Noise, the Dark Tunnel, Out of the Body, Meeting Others, the Being of Light, the Review, the Border of Limit, Coming Back, Telling Others, Effects on Lives. Moody suggests that the surprising similarity in reports, the uniform experience of death as inviting (at least when one gets close), and the feeling of welcome at entrance and anger at being drawn back, show the probability of life after life.

One who works in the medical establishment can appreciate the healthy corrective found in the Moody observations and conclusions. For decades, medicine has been obsessed with physical vitality, psychological adjustment, and prolongation of life. Motivated by an understanding of death as enemy, medicine has gotten itself into an unfortunate bind where it is often accused, quite rightly, of being a force that generates illness. Ivan Illich sees the problem of iatrogenic disease (doctor-made) as a major crisis in our quest for health. A recent study of leukemia and other blood and lymphatic cancers concluded that a major cause of cancer was cancer treatment.

Moody's studies argue that death is not the perverse, inimical force that we have made it to be. Thus his studies collapse the vital tension between the will to live and the will to die. The danger of the life after life ideology is not only the defective theology, it is the risk that people might welcome, hasten, and perhaps even inflict death. The flurry of "natural death" acts, the more permissive conscience regarding abortion, the discussion of limits to care—all ring an ominous tone. This is especially true when such public policies are built on a defective theology of human life.

The Search for Physical Immortality

The yearning for an indefinite prolongation of life has long tantalized people. The search for the golden age or for the fountain of youth was actually a search for immortality. And the search still continues.

In the nineteenth century, Ludwig Feuerbach began to probe the notion of physical immortality.

> Immortal life is the life which exists for its own sake, and contains its own aim and purpose in itself—immortal life is the full life, rich in contents. . . . Every moment of life is of infinite importance and significance, for its own sake, posited by itself and fulfilled in itself, an unlimited affirmation of its own self; every moment of life is like a draught which empties completely the cup of infinity, which like the cup of Oberon miraculously fills itself again and again. . . . Life is music, and every moment is a melody, or a sound full of deep feeling . . . the sounds of music pass away, but each sound has meaning as a sound, and before this inner significance, the "soul" of the sound, transitoriness recedes as something unimportant and inconsequential.[105]

Today a lively quest goes on to secure immortality on a nonreligious basis. Many people who cannot believe in life after death believe that the legacy one leaves through works, family, and influence, is a lasting monument, a kind of immortality. Another approach is to search for *physical* immortality. I received this morning my copy of the newsletter of The Committee to Abolish Death. To survey this effort, let us examine the subject of anabiosis (returning to life) and immortality.

Reflection: *Anabiosis and Immortality:*[106]

Roger Ornsten, a five-year-old Norwegian boy, fell into an icy river in 1962 and drowned. He was under water for 22 minutes and his body temperature fell below 75°F which doctors say prevented swift deterioration of his brain. Although apparently dead on arrival at the hospital, Dr. Tone Kvittingen, who reports the incident in the *British Medical Journal* [107], applied artificial respiration with a tube down the windpipe, and rhythmic pressure on the chest to force blood circulation. Although nearly two hours had elapsed without a heartbeat, resuscitation continued, including exchange blood transfusions. Natural heartbeat suddenly resumed, and although Roger remained unconscious for six weeks he now is completely recovered with only slight impairment of muscular coordination and peripheral vision. This dramatic recovery has often been repeated with new cardiopulmonary resuscitation techniques.

The unique element in this case—hypothermia, or cooling—is the subject of a thrilling novel by Nikolai Amosoff, the Russian cardiovascular surgeon. Although the original full text did not pass Soviet censorship, the abbreviated version was published under the title *Notes From the Future*.

The novel raises several important issues that are now surfacing in our culture, all of which are aspects of the quest for immortality. In recent years a vast literature—factual, semi-fictional and fictional—has emerged on this same question. Previously the theme had been limited to poetry, science fiction and Rod Serling. Now it appears in scientific literature as well. Robert Ettinger's *The Prospect of Immortality* appeared in 1964; Lucy Kavaler's *Freezing Point: Cold as a Matter of Life and Death* in 1970. In the interim, numerous studies, including Herman Kahn's *The Year 2000* and Gordon Taylor's *The Biological Time Bomb*, have announced the possibility of human hibernation in order to cure disease and increase longevity.

I propose to approach the issue of anabiosis and immortality by first reviewing the *Notes from the Future*, noting particularly the themes and value statements of the Russian scientist. Second, the issues surrounding cryogenics, hibernation and evolution and immortality will be sketched. Finally reflection will be offered from the perspective of a religious vision of life.

Notes from the Future is the diary of Ivan Nikolaevich, physiologist and cyberneticist in a Moscow Institute. The year is 1969. His team is developing mathematical formulae and mechanical models to program and reduplicate human systems. Ivan discovers he has leukemia. Therefore he reorganizes his Institute into an anabiosis laboratory. The sarcophagus is built. It resembles the astronaut capsules in the film *2001: A Space Odyssey*. All body systems are sustained mechanically. The experimentation schedule is intensified. Five dogs are cooled down to the point where metabolism grinds slowly toward the zero point. After brief hibernation, they are resuscitated. All the dogs die, for reasons other than the anabiosis, of course. Despite these failures, Ivan will now submit himself to the experiment:

> "Why not? Lower organisms undergo successful suspended animation, mammals hibernate, why not man? The human body is more complex it is true. But we have new methods, chemicals, plasma, artificial organs, support devices. Granted the awakening is a problem—but we may assume science will discover this while I'm asleep? If not, what has been lost?"

Slowly life is drained from Ivan's body, his blood is replaced with plasma, mechanical organs take over, many probes are inserted into his body—the plexiglass pressure chamber is locked in. So ends Part One of *Notes*.

It is now February 20, 1991. Ivan has been in the sarcophagus 22 years. The cure for leukemia has been discovered. Ivan is rejuvenated and comes back for "a second hundred years." He is a showpiece. He reads the report of his "awakening."

> "The process itself has been thoroughly worked out. There is a set of mechanisms taking care of all bodily functions. It is governed by the central electronic computer, based on the exact model of the organism. . . . The mechanical aids cease operating

just as soon as the various organs start functioning. . . .The entire system has been thoroughly tested on animals and during space flights. It will probably be used for the first manned flight to Pluto" *(Notes,* p. 207).

The world has been completely computerized during his absence. "The world of information, the world of models," he cries, "is the true God of the universe." He visits New York and Tokyo. The cities are beautiful; the little industrial ugliness that remains has been moved to the countryside. The deviant, the criminal and the insane are exiled to Valim—another world in the far reaches of space. The world is sterile, predictable and peaceful in a benign sense of that word.

After his psychological rehabilitation (psychologists are the pastors and priests of the new society, *Notes* p. 303), Ivan launches an Immortality Institute. His research is focused on immortality defined as "greatly extended longevity," or elsewhere as "the indefinite lengthening of the span of human life."

"What must I do to further my work in this sphere?" asks Ivan. "First of all, make research inquiries into the following questions:

1. Is the process of aging programmed in the genes?
2. What are the 'molecular obstacles' causing the wear and tear of the human body?
3. The comparative importance of the 'outward obstacles' coming from the air, nourishment, et cetera, and the 'internal' ones arising from functional disturbances of the internal organs of the body.
4. What are the existing materials for drawing a pattern-of-aging scheme—weak links in cells, organs and regulating systems—the endocrine glands and the nervous system?
5. What are the wear 'loads' resulting from improper nourishment?

The methods: physiology, molecular biology, models on the cell and organ levels.

Possible ways of improving longevity: regulated nourishment from birth; elimination of destructive factors on the physical and emotional planes; repair work—including cell and organ replacement.

It is quite possible, I think, to stretch the average span of human life to 120-150 years. But this is not yet immortality. Besides the brain usually begins to deteriorate earlier. Hence, another problem: the use of an artificial brain in man's everyday activity. After all, intellect is the focal point of man's well-being. Man is alive for as long as his brain functions—and the artificial brain can start helping the natural one early in life, thus preserving it from undue wear. To achieve even proper research into these spheres one needs large financial backing, high-grade personnel, and a proper organization. What I need is the Immortality Institute. No more and no less." [108]

Amosoff has been soundly scolded by his scientific colleagues for writing "unscientific fiction." His answer: "the only unscientific thing in science is calling anything unscientific." Scientists here in our center who know Amosoff remark on the unusual way he reports at a scientific meeting. He begins with the customary clinical reporting, then moves to visionary, futuristic discourse, remarked one of his colleagues. Amosoff told his translator in Moscow, "There is nothing impossible for modern science. Saints used to produce miracles, and artists dreams. Now it is the scientists' turn." [109]

An interesting constellation of values is presented in Amosoff's writing:

(1) He comes across as a reconstructed Marxist-humanist. He has lost the orthodox drive to obliterate the notion of immortality from human consciousness. The notion of earthly immortality is in fact encouraged by Amosoff.

(2) Amosoff speaks through the psychologist who believes that universal happiness can be created by improving human nature. This can be managed by social and chemical manipulation. After his second lover is killed in a rape-murder, he is spared acute grief through dream therapy.

(3) He exhibits a simple passion for human love and camaraderie through his relationship with Liuba and Anna, his lover-

companions, as well as to the team of scientists at the Institute. Ivan is the autobiographical projection of Amosoff who revels in the joy of human kindness, pleasure in the simple things of life, exhilaration in high vocational purpose.

(4) He exhibits a cautiously optimistic attitude toward technology. It enables people to remain human, yet it should not be taken too seriously. There is a marvelous passage where he describes the mechanical "nanny" that takes his beloved child from him at night. Anna wants to nurse the child, but they submit to the superiority of the machine:

> I tell Anna to stop breast-feeding her. This is old-fashioned and completely unnecessary. Pediatricians and chemists compose formulas far superior to mother's milk. More nourishing and tastier. But Anna doesn't believe it. Now, it is Masha herself who refuses the breast. She is more intelligent than her learned mother.
>
> The science of child-raising has advanced spectacularly. Even before Anna and Masha came home from the clinic, they had delivered to our place a fantastic contraption—the "automatic nanny." I studied it the whole night, reading instructions and working controls. (And how do less educated people handle it?)
>
> The machine does everything: changes rubber pads the moment they get wet, puts the child to sleep, regulates the temperature inside the crib. And, most important, educates. They have found out that the cortex cells develop faster if they are exercised from birth. There is a whole built-in program—with variations. First, the child is shown splotches of color, to train attention. Then sounds; then toys. And it feeds the child in the morning. You set the machine in the evening, and no more trouble.
>
> But not with us. Anna does not believe in the machine and jumps out of bed if Masha as much as stirs in her sleep. If the machine had emotions, it would be annoyed. I know I am.[110]

Several issues are raised at this point such as the general areas of cryogenics and anabiosis. In a culture that is increasingly secular and sensate, the quest for long, full life will be strong.

Herman Kahn, in his forecast of *The Year 2000*, sees this emergent ethos expressed through numerous impending life extension and hibernation procedures.

In Table 23 on "One Hundred Mechanical Innovations" very likely in the last third of the twentieth century he lists:

#14 Extensive use of cyborg techniques (mechanical aids or substitutes for human organs, senses, links or other components.)

#19 Human hibernation for short periods (hours or days) for medical purposes.

#35 Human hibernation for relatively extensive periods (months to years.)

#61 Widespread use of cryogenics.

In his Table 19 he lists possibilities which are less likely but nevertheless important:

#8 Suspended animation for years or centuries.

#13 Major rejuvenation and/or significant extension of vigor and life span, say 100-150 years.

Then in Table 20 he lists ten far-out possibilities:

1 Life expectancy extended to substantially more than 150 years (immortality?)

#9 Life time immunization against practically all diseases.[111]

Cryosurgery is now widespread; cryobiology is increasing in use. Sperm, for example, have been frozen for months, remaining viable to impregnate an egg. We probably hope such esoteric research will go slowly until we have time to understand it better. But it is the nature of such research to surge forward.

The issue of hibernation and evolution deserves note. It is a strange twist of history that cryogenic capacity has emerged at the very moment of population crisis. We can begin to learn to extend life only now when the imperative is to limit population. The latter imperative requires both decreasing birthrate and maintaining steady death rate unless we choose to have a society dominated by the elderly, feeble and maimed that Muller and others have warned us of.

Extensive cryogenics could indeed rupture the evolutionary process. The Russian cyberneticist, Victor Pekelis, expresses this radical paradox: "The maximum metabolic stability—immortality —would mean an end of all evolution." [112] In other words, from the perspective of biological evolution man must die in order that he might live.

Another issue is quantity vs. quality of life. Abnormal longevity can be a horrifying prospect if you stop to think about it. And what of the social dimension? What entitles some few to seek a postponed deadline, while for others the basic quality of life goes unfulfilled? Dr. King was prophetic in his last sermon in Memphis when he pondered long life, yet chose God's will.

Finally, I'm wondering how a faithful person can help society make decisions and form policy on these issues. Two things come to mind: the prophetic and priestly elements in life. The *prophetic* task would prompt us to question the assumption that we are dealing with some "progressive inevitability" which cannot be stopped. Listen to Robert Ettinger:

> The theologians in good time will decide on all such questions. Or rather, several schools of theologians will each evolve a whole series of accommodations to the developing insights of science and the developing pressures of society, in the usual way.[113]

Oppenheimer felt the tragedy of the scientific assumption that what is "technically sweet becomes irrestible." What we can do, we must do. Perhaps the task of faithful people today is to remind us of our mortality. The quest is noble—not for immortality but for wholeness. We are born to die. The power of technology, as Amosoff suggests, merely throws us back to the meaning of the personal. As C. P. Snow reflected on the moon landing, "the universe is vacant. The only life we shall ever meet will be our own." [114] Theologically discerned, our mortality—our conditionedness—is the clue to our destiny.

The *priestly* task says No! to artificial life, and Yes! to that which affirms natural life and value. This mood asserts that human life has meaning and destiny. This significance is anchored in the cosmic process of renewal that we call redemption. This constructive task is going to demand two things of responsible people in the years ahead. Time immemorial has called us to affirm life in the midst of death. Now the future calls us to affirm life in the midst of *life*.

VII

Hospices
and Care for the Dying

T HE ONLY THING MORE COURAGEOUS than the way in which he lived his life was the manner in which he left it" (President Jimmy Carter, January 14, 1978). At 9:25 P.M., January 13, Hubert Horatio Humphrey died at his home in Waverly, Minnesota. He had wanted to stay in Washington through the Christmas holidays. He decided, however, in consultation with his protege, Vice President Walter Mondale, to go home. "He showed us all how to die with dignity, with courage, with spirit and with meaning," reflected Mondale. He fought the battle with cancer for four years. Surgery, radiation, even experimental therapy were used. Underneath it all he was buoyed up by a zest for life, an energetic hope, tempered by a realistic acceptance. Together these impulses blended into a couragous and even humorous serenity.

His will to live was strong. He possessed an unflagging spirit. When the Minnesota Vikings dropped by on their way to an NFL playoff game, he almost packed his bags and went along. He wanted to exhaust the opportunity of each moment to serve others. He refused to take mind-numbing painkillers. In his last hours he composed an appeal to Israeli Prime Minister Begin to remain flexible in Middle East negotiations. He drafted a civil rights statement urging the nation to bridge the "huge valley of shame" separating black and white America.

His willingness to die was also there in healthy tension. After a malignant bladder tumor had been removed in 1974 he became "quite philosophical" about the possibility that he might not be cured. "What can be done by medicine, surgery or radiation, I'll have it. And if it can't be, then I'll have had it, you know. And that's it. And I really don't worry about it. I have something else to do" (New York Times, January 15, 1978, p. 26). Celebration and humor were to mark his funeral. "The last time we had a service this long," eulogized his pastor, "was when Hubert last preached."

He elected not to have last ditch, all holds barred therapy and life-support. He went home to die. With Muriel and family at his side, and his white dog at his feet, he took his leave.

In addition to the renewed interest in dying at home, innovative medical work in the area of caring for the dying is the popularization of the hospice idea by Dr. Cicely Saunders. St. Christopher's Hospice in London (Sydenham) is an example of tender and humane care for dying persons that is now being emulated around the world. An ancient idea, the hospice has served human communities down through the ages of Christian civilization. But the modern health movement symbolized by the clinical hospital, repudiated the hospice tradition.

Now the idea is being revived. Rather than "death houses" with narcotized, bedridden, depressed patients, the new programs seek to engage patients, family, staff, and community into a caring fellowship of comfort and affirmation as individuals go toward death. Though it originated outside the National Health Services in England, it is now supported by both public and private funds. In the United States many cities are now activating, or at least planning, hospices to serve their terminally ill people.

The environments are natural, humane, and personal. The patient is greeted on arrival and given his own bed. There are family rooms with open spaces for group activities. The beds are simple and low. Visiting hours are liberal. There is a strong emphasis on touch, personal conversation, contact, visiting, and children. Everyday clothes and accustomed surroundings are maintained. There is not a great emphasis on diagnostic tests, X-rays, lab reports, innovative therapeutics, etc. Patients are there to be comforted, relieved of their pain, and surrounded with concern and conviviality as death approaches.

There are always many people milling around. Birthday parties, family celebrations, joking with staff and volunteers is commonplace. The privacy of the patient, especially the desire to be left alone to one's reflection and prayer, is honored. In addition to therapeutic management, the patient's emotional, spiritual, and social needs are sensitively attended.

Various medications are tailored to the particular needs of patients, such as Brompton's mixture, diamorphine (heroin) and other effective painkillers. Anti-anxiety drugs and a variety of other measures help make pain as meaningful and bearable as possible. Life support mechanisms are seldom used and resuscitation is rarely employed. Chapel services are part of the daily life of the community and the deep moral and spiritual values of persons are honored and nurtured. The patients do not die alone. They are surrounded by family and those workers who have become their friends.[115]

Dr. Donald McCarthy, a leading Catholic theologian, has urged that the hospice movement may be the answer to our increasing perplexity regarding euthanasia.[116] There is a convergence of concerns in our world today. First, the patient does not wish to have anything and everything done to him to prolong his life. Where there is chance for recovery, certainly we hope medicine will be heroic and successful. Where the only value medical care can serve is prolongation of the dying process, many individuals will choose to let nature take its course. The many persons who have recorded "living wills" or "Catholic Affirmations of Life" have indicated the preference for care rather than experimentation.

Ultimately what we need are a variety of institutions and settings where one can die with the style and meaning desired. Jane Brody, the medicine writer for the *New York Times*, tells how "Seth Died at Home." [117]

> "Seth died cuddled in our arms before a blazing fire in utter quiet and peace. We have such good feelings about the peace of that moment that it has been immeasurably easier to deal with this reality."
>
> Seth was 19 months old when he died of leukemia. His father wrote the words quoted above in a letter to Ida Marie Martinson, associate professor and director of research at the University of Minnesota School of Nursing, Minneapolis. It was her program that made it possible for the family to care for Seth at home in the final days of his illness. At a recent American Cancer Society seminar, Martinson described the program. Designed for children with cancer for whom there is no longer any hope of cure, it has shown in less than a year that the care of a dying child at home is feasible and makes the family's psychological adjustment easier. A nurse is on call 24 hours a day if needed, but the parents are the "primary care" givers.
>
> The experience helps parents to realize they have done all they could. It alleviates guilt feelings, and enables the family to cope better afterward, Professor Martinson found. "Too often," she said, "in the hospital setting, health professions get between the dying child and his family." But at home, most of the children have chosen to die in the living room with their families nearby.

Postscript

A SIMPLE THESIS has meandered through the observations, reflections and meditations of this book. I have argued that at the depths of life, truth is found in paradox. The motif comes from Christian theology, as anyone will recognize. One cannot improve on Chesterton's summary:

> Paganism declared that virtue was in a balance; Christianity declared it was in a conflict: the collision of two passions apparently opposite. Of course they were not really inconsistent; but they were such that it was hard to hold simultaneously. Let us follow for a moment the clue of the martyr and the suicide; and take the case of courage. No quality has ever so much addled the brains and tangled the definitions of merely rational sages. Courage is almost a contradiction in terms. It means a strong desire to live taking the form of a readiness to die. "He that will lose his life, the same shall save it," is not a piece of mysticism for saints and heroes. It is a piece of everyday advice for sailors or mountaineers. It might be printed in an Alpine guide or a drill book. This paradox is the whole principle of courage; even of quite earthly or quite brutal courage.[118]

Healthful and moral living in the face of inevitable death creates a vital tension. The authentic will to live contains a willingness to die. A will to die is morbid unless it is tempered by hope. Holding the will to live and the willingness to die in tension is the genius that makes us human. It saves us from cynicism. It asserts that absurdity and annihilation are impossible in a world sustained by a gracious providence.

Maintenance of this tension is crucial to a recovery of personal happiness and societal sanity in a world obsessed with life because of its fear of death. Every moral issue in medicine draws out this concern. Abortion, euthanasia, human experimentation, the prolongation of life through artificial life-supports—all these are issues that test our philosophies, our theologies, and our ethics regarding death. The personal quest for a good death and the societal search for natural death remain the primary moral tasks of our time.

Notes

1. "Brother Held in Apparent Mercy Killing" *New York Times* (June 23, 1973) 35; and "Jersey Slayer of Paralyzed Brother in Hospital Called a Hero and a Villain by Shore Neighbors" *New York Times* (June 24, 1973) 29.
2. Robert Veatch, *Death, Dying and the Biological Revolution: Our Last Quest for Responsibility* (New Haven: Yale University Press, 1976).
3. New York Review of Books. Thomas McKeown, *The Modern Rise of Population* (Academic, 1976).
4. Edwin S. Schneidman, *Deaths of Man* (Baltimore: Penguin, 1974) 124.
5. Geoffrey Gorer, *Death, Grief and Mourning* (Garden City, N.Y., Doubleday, 1965).
6. Malcolm Muggeridge, *The Observer* (Feb. 20, 1970).
7. Richard Kalish, "Some Variables in Death Attitudes" in *Death and Identity,* Robert Fulton, ed. (New York: John Wiley and Sons, 1965).
8. C. S. Lewis, *A Grief Observed* (Boston: Seabury, 1963) 57.
9. Alexandre Koyéve, *Introduction à la Lecture de Hegel,* 5th ed. (Paris: Gallimard, 1947) 573.
10. See for example Elisabeth Kübler-Ross, *On Death and Dying* (New York: Macmillan, 1969) and Raymond A. Moody, Jr. *Life After Life* (New York: Bantam, 1975).
11. See John Hick, *Death and Eternal Life* (New York: Harper & Row, 1976).
12. Elisabeth Kübler-Ross, *On Death and Dying.* (New York: Macmillan, 1969).

135

13. Becker won the Pulitzer Prize for his book *The Denial of Death.* (Free Press, 1973). A moving interview with Sam Keen on Becker's deathbed (Psychology Today, April, 1974) shows the vibrant quality of this dialogical perception of meaning.

14. Harvey Bates "Letters from Ernest" in *Christian Century* (March 9, 1977), 224.

15. Avery Weisman, and Thomas Hackett, "The Dying Patient," *Forest Hospital Publications,* 1:16-21, 1962.

16. John Donne, "Death Be Not Proud."

17. Emily Dickinson, "1599" *An Emily Dickinson Sampler* (Logan, Iowa; The Perfection Form Company) 56. (Poem written about 1880.)

18. This is modified from a paper by Alex M. Capron and Leon R. Kass "A Statutory Definition of the Standards for Determining Human Death: An Appraisal and a Proposal" *University of Pennsylvania Law Review* 121 (November, 1972) 87-118.

19. This is adapted from Harvard Medical School, Ad Hoc Committee of the Harvard Medical School to Examine the Definition of Brain Death, "A Definition of Irreversible Coma" *Journal of the American Medical Association.* 205 (1968) 337-340.

20. Montague Lane, et al., "The Medical Determination of Death," privately distributed paper, March 18, 1977.

21. Special Article, "Optimum Care for Hopelessly Ill Patients" A Report of the Clinical Care Committee of the Massachusetts General Hospital, *New England Journal of Medicine* (August 12, 1976, Vol. 295, No. 7), 362ff.

22. Herman Feifel, et al., "Physicians Consider Death" *Proceedings of the Annual Convention of the American Psychological Association,* 1967.

23. See Elisabeth Kübler-Ross, *Questions and Answers on Death and Dying* (New York: Macmillan, 1974).

24. See Kenneth Vaux, *This Mortal Coil: The Meaning of Health and Disease* (Harper & Row, 1977).

25. P. Matussek, *Metaphysische Probleme` der Medizin* (Berlin/Heidelberg: Springer, 1948) 126.

26. John Donne, *Devotions* (Chapter Outline).

27. William Easson, "The Lazarus Syndrome in Childhood" *Medical Insight,* (Vol. 4, Nov. 1972) 47ff. See also *The Dying Child* (Springfield, Ill.: C. C. Thomas, 1970).

28. Erik Erikson, "Protest and Affirmation" in *Harvard Medical Bulletin,* (Fall, 1972) 31.

29. Lewis, 34.

30. Kerr L. White, "Life and Death in Medicine" *Scientific American* (September 1973, Vol. 229, No. 3) 25.

31. Robert Morrison, "Death: Process or Event" *Science* (August 1971), 108.

32. Robert Morrison, "Darwinism: Foundation for an Ethical System" *Zygon* (December 1966, Vol. 1, No. 4), 349.

33. William McNeill, *Plagues and Peoples* (New York: Anchor-Double-day, 1976) 254.
34. McNeill, 282.
35. Joseph Fletcher, "The 'Right' to Live and the 'Right' to Die" in Marvin Kohl, ed., *Beneficient Euthanasia* (Buffalo, New York: Prometheus, 1975) 47.
36. Stewart Wolf, et al., "Roseto Revisited: Further Data on the Incidence of Myocardial Infarction in Roseto and Neighboring Pennsylvania Communities" *Transactions of the American Clinical and Climatological Association* (Vol. 85, 1973).
37. Michael DeBakey, "The Medical Prognosis: Favorable, Treatable, Curable" *Saturday Review World* (August 24, 1974), 46.
38. T. S. Eliot, *Four Quartets* (New York: Harcourt, Brace, 1968) 79.
39. Kenneth Vaux, "Ethics of Medicine and the Spirit of Western Culture" *The New York Times* (Friday, January 31, 1975), 33.
40. Theodosius Dobzhansky, "An Essay on Religion, Death and Evolutionary Adaption," *Zygon* (Vol. 1, No. 4, December, 1966), 320-324.
41. Martin Luther, *Luther's Works*, Vol. 13 (Philadelphia: Fortress, 1955) 94, quoted in Helmut Thielicke, *Death and Life* (Philadelphia: Fortress, 1970) 151.
42. Daniel Callahan, "The Sanctity of Life," in Donald R. Cutler, ed. *The Religious Situation: 1969* (Boston: Beacon, 1969) 297ff.
43. The ultimate consequences of this kind of system are requirements that the physician be the government's arm of punishment (i.e., Nazi Germany; Lybia today where physicians must amputate hands for convicted shoplifters), or surveillance (i.e. dermatologists circulating in their literature an F.B.I. poster of a man wanted with a rare skin disorder).
44. Schneidman, 51.
45. Hugh P. Whitt, et al., "Religion, Economic Development and Lethal Aggression," *American Sociological Review* (1972, Vol. 37 April), 193-201.
46. Max Weber, *The Protestant Ethic and the Spirit of Capitalism* (New York: Scribners, 1958).
47. Leonard Berkowitz, *Aggression: A Social-Psychological Analysis* (New York: McGraw Hill, 1962).
48. Emile Durkheim *Le Suicide* (Paris: Felix- Alcan, 1897).
49. Whitt, 196.
50. J. Riviere, "The Unconscious Fantasy of an Inner World Effected in Examples from English Literature" *International Journal of Psychoanalysis*, 11, 160-172.
51. Robert M. Pirsig, *Zen and the Art of Motorcycle Maintenance* (New York: Bantam, 1974) 26.
52. C. S. Lewis, "The Caves of Venus" from *The World's Last Night and Other Essays* (New York: Harcourt, Brace and World, 1962) 6.
53. Karl Marx, "Economic and Philosophical Manuscripts" in Erich Fromm *Marx's Concept of Man* (New York: Ungar, 1961) 95.
54. Don Shriver, "An Ethic for Growth," 1974, unpublished paper.

55. Herman Daly, ed., *Toward a Steady State Economy* (San Francisco: W. H. Freeman, 1973) 151.
56. E.M.I. Records. Printed and made in Great Britain by Garrod & Lofthouse Ltd.
57. See Jan van Eys, ed., *The Truly Cured Child* (Baltimore: University Park Press, 1977).
58. Thomas Hardy, *Jude the Obscure* (New York, 1895) 406.
59. Condorcet, "Outline of the Progress of the Human Mind." Quoted in Jacques Choron, *Death and Western Thought* (New York: Collier, 1963) 135.
60. The death of a child has always been a heart-wrenching experience. Yet in previous centuries the death of children was expected, if not seen as somehow natural or timely. The ancient prayer "If I should die before I wake" was not idle repetition. The child could and often did perish during the night. Rousseau could write in 1762, "Although we know approximately the limits of human life and our chance of attaining these limits, nothing is more uncertain than the length of the life of any of us. Very few reach old age. The chief risks occur at the beginning of life; the shorter our past life, the less we hope to live. Of all the children who are born scarcely one half reach adolescence, and it is very likely your pupil will not live to be a man." Jean Jacques Rosseau, *Emil* (New York: Dutton, 1966) 42.
61. Herbert Marcuse, "The Ideology of Death" in Herman Feifel, *The Meaning of Death* (New York: McGraw Hill, 1959) 69.
62. Ernst Bloch, *Das Prinzip Hoffnung* (Frankfurt: Suhrkamp, 1959) 1389.
63. T. W. Adorno, *Jargon der Eigenthchkeit* (Frankfurt: Suhrkamp, 1964) 130.
64. W. Fuchs, *Todesbilder in der Modernen Gesellschaft* (Frankfurt: Suhrkamp, 1969) 179.
65. Romano Guardini, *Rainer Maria Rilke's Deutung des Daseins* (Munich: Kosel, 1961) 398.
66. Blaise Pascal, quoted in Choron, 119.
67. Gabriel Marcel, quoted in M. M. Davy, *Un Philosophe Itinerant: Gabriel Marcel* (Paris: Flammarson, 1959) 316.
68. Richard Bailey, "Economic and Social Costs of Death" in *The Dying Patient,* ed. Orville G. Brim, Jr. et al., (New York: Russell Sage Foundation, 1970).
69. Thornton Wilder, *Bridge of San Luis Rey* (New York: Harper & Row, 1967).
70. "Terminally Ill Allowed Natural Death," *The Charlotte Observer,* (Wed., June 29, 1977) 1.
71. Ivan Illich, "The Political Uses of Natural Death," *Hastings Center Studies* (January 1974, Vol. 2, No. 1) 8.
72. Illich, 17.
73. See Karen Lebacqz, "Contemporary on Natural Death," *Hastings Center Report* (April 1977) 14.

74. Richard A. McCormick and Andre E. Hellegers, "Legislation and the Living Will," *America* (March 12, 1977) 213.
75. Quoted in *Montaigne Por Lui-meme,* translated by Francis Jeanson (Paris: Editions du Seuil, 1951) 45.
76. Galen, "The Use of Limbs: Section 3," *On the Natural Faculties.* (Cambridge: Harvard University Press, 1948).
77. Blackstone, *Commentary of the Law of England.* Book 4, Chapter 14.
78. *On Dying Well: An Anglican Contribution to the Debate on Euthanasia* (London: Church Information Office, 1975).
79. Daniel Callahan "On Defining Natural Death," *Hastings Center Report* (June 1977) 33.
80. *John Hick, Death and Eternal Life* (New York: Harper and Row, 1975).
81. Hick, 207.
82. Anselm, *Cur Deus Homo?* Book 2, Ch. 2.
83. J. E. Meyer, *Death and Neurosis* (New York: International Universities Press, 1975) 96.
84. Homer, *Odyssey,* XI, 488-491.
85. Quoted in A. E. Taylor, *Plato: The Man and His Work* (New York: Meridian 1956) 183-208.
86. Plotinus, *Enneads IV,* 8, 1, Stephen McKenna Trans. (London: Faber, 1957).
87. Schelling, *Gesammelte Werke.* 1856-1861, Bk. 2, 248ff.
88. Raymond A. Moody, Jr., *Life After Life* (New York: Bantam, 1977).
89. Moody, 160.
90. Antigone in *The Oedipus Plays of Sophocles.* Trans. Paul Roche (New York: Mentor, 1958) 180, 181.
91. Teilhard de Chardin, *Le Milieu Divin* (London: Collins, 1960) 69.
92. G. K. Chesterton, *Orthodoxy* (London: Collins, 1908) 91-92.
93. Lewis, *A Grief Observed* 25.
94. Lucien Levy-Bruhl, *Primitive Mentality* (New York: Macmillan, 1923) See Chap. 1.
95. Louis I. Dublin, *Factbook on Man—From Birth to Death* (New York: Macmillan, 1965) 394.
96. Homer, *Odyssey,* Translated: Lang, Leaf, and Myers. (New York: St. Martins, 1961, Book IV) II, 560ff.
97. Quoted in S. G. F. Brandon, *The Judgment of the Dead* (New York: Scribners, 1969) 9.
98. See *The Book of the Dead* (Egyptian), British Museum, London, 1933. For a full discussion of this development, see Hick, 50ff.
99. Quoted in A. S. Peake, ed., *The People and the Book* (London: Oxford, 1925) 362.
100. Max Scheler, "Tod und Fortleben" in *Schriften aus dem Nachlass* (Berne: Franke, 1933, Vol. 1) 45.
101. Oscar Cullman, "Immortality of the Soul or Resurrection of the Dead?" in *Immortality and Resurrection,* ed. Krister Stendahl. (New York: Macmillan, 1965) 26-27.

102. Paul Goodman, *Growing Up Absurd* (New York: Random House, 1960).
103. Hans Morgenthau, "Death in the Nuclear Age" in Nathan Scott, ed., *The Modern Vision of Death* (Richmond, Va.: John Knox, 1967) 73.
104. Moody, *Life After Life*.
105. Ludwig Feuerbach, *Theoretische Seelenkrankheit*, in *Saemmtliche Werke*, Vol. X. (Leipzig, 1847-1866) 88.
106. See the article by Azriel Rosenfeld, "Refrigeration, Resuscitation and Resurrection," in *Tradition*, (9, No. 3, 1967) 82-95.
107. T. D. Kvittingen and A. Naess, "Recovery from Drowning in Fresh Water," *British Medical Journal*, May 18, 1963.
108. Nikolai Amosoff, *Notes From the Future* (New York: Simon and Schuster, 1969) 291-292.
109. *Look*, (July 7, 1970) 58.
110. Amosoff, 317.
111. Herman Kahn and Anthony T. Wiener, *The Year 2000* (New York: Macmillan, 1967) 53ff.
112. *Look*, 65.
113. Robert Ettinger, *The Prospect of Immortality* (New York: McFadden, 1966).
114. *Look*, (August 26, 1969) 7.
115. Leonard M. Liegner, "St. Christopher's Hospice, 1974—Care of the Dying Patient," *Journal of the American Medical Association*, (Dec. 8, 1975, Vol. 234, No. 10) 1047ff.
116. Donald C. McCarthy, "Should Catholic Hospitals Sponsor Hospices?" *Hospital Progress*, (December, 1976) 61ff.
117. Jane E. Brody, "Seth Died at Home," *The New York Times*, quoted in The Reader's Digest, (August, 1977) 122.
118. Chesterton, 91.

Bibliography

Alvarez, A. *The Savage God: A Study of Suicide*. New York: Random House, 1972.

Aries, Philippe. *Western Attitudes Toward Death: From the Middle Ages to the Present*. Translated by Patricia M. Ranum, Baltimore: Johns Hopkins, 1974.

Becker, Ernest. *The Denial of Death*. New York: Free Press, 1973.

Brim, Orville G., Jr., et al., eds. *The Dying Patient*. New York: Russell Sage Foundation, 1970.

Cartwright, Ann, et al. *Life Before Death*. London: Routledge and Kegan Paul, 1973.

Catholic Hospital Association. *Christian Affirmation of Life*. St. Louis: Catholic Hospital Association, 1974.

Choron, Jacques. *Death and Western Thought*. New York: Collier 1973.

———. *Suicide,* New York: Scribners, 1972.

Crane, Diana. *The Social Aspects of the Prolongation of Life*. Social Science Frontiers. New York: Russell Sage Foundation, 1969.

Cutler, Donald, ed. *Updating Life and Death*. Boston: Beacon, 1969.

Douglas, J. D. *The Social Meaning of Suicide*. Princeton: Princeton University Press, 1967.

Downing, A. B. *Euthanasia and the Right to Die*. New York: Humanities, 1970.

Durkheim, E. *Suicide*. Glencoe, Ill.: Free Press, 1951.

Ettinger, Robert. *The Prospect of Immortality*. New York: MacFadden, 1966.

Farberow, N. L. and Shneidman, E. S., eds. *The Cry for Help*. New York: McGraw-Hill, 1961.

141

Gould, Jonathan and Craigmyle, Lord, eds. *Your Death Warrant? The Implications of Euthanasia*. New York: Arlington House, 1973.

Hendin, David. *Death as a Fact of Life*. New York: Norton, 1973.

Hick, John. *Death and Eternal Life*. New York: Harper & Row, 1976.

Illich, Ivan. *Medical Nemesis*. New York: Pantheon, 1976.

Kluge, Eike-Henner W. *The Practice of Death*. New Haven: Yale University Press, 1975.

Kohl, Marvin, ed. *Beneficent Euthanasia*. Buffalo, N.Y.: Prometheus, 1975.

Kübler-Ross, Elisabeth. *Death: The Final Stage of Growth*. Englewood Cliffs, N.J.: Prentice-Hall, 1975.

————. *On Death and Dying*. New York: Macmillan, 1969.

Lewis, C. S. *A Grief Observed*. Boston: Beacon, 1960.

Lifton, Robert Jay and Olson, Eric. *Living and Dying*. New York: Praeger, 1974.

Mack, Arien, ed. *Death in the American Experience*. New York: Schocken, 1973.

Maguire, Daniel C. *Death by Choice*. Garden City, N.Y.: Doubleday, 1974.

Mannes, Marya. *The Case for the Good Death*. New York: Morrow, 1974.

McEllhenney, John Galen. *Cutting the Monkey Rope*, Valley Forge, Pa.: Judson, 1973.

Meyer, J. E. *Death and Neurosis*. New York: International Universities Press, 1975.

Moody, Raymond A. Jr. *Life After Life*. New York: Bantam, 1977.

Morison, Robert S. "Dying." *Scientific American* 229 (September, 1973), 55-62.

Neale, Robert E. *The Art of Dying*. New York: Harper & Row, 1973.

Pearson, Leonard, ed. *Death and Dying: Current Issues in the Treatment of the Dying Person*. Cleveland: Case-Western Reserve University Press, 1969.

Ramsey, Paul. *The Patient as Person*. New Haven: Yale University Press, 1970.

Riemer, Jack, ed. *Jewish Reflections on Death*. New York: Schocken, 1975.

Roslansky, John D., ed. *The End of Life*. New York: Fleet Academic Editions, 1973.

Shneidman, Edwin S. *Deaths of Man*. New York: Quadrangle, 1973.

Solzhenitsyn, A. *Cancer Ward*. New York: Bantam, 1969.

Tolstoy, Leo. *Death of Ivan Illyich*. New York: Signet (New American Library), 1960.

Toynbee, Arnold, et al. *Man's Concern with Death*. New York: McGraw-Hill, 1968.

Vaux, Kenneth. *This Mortal Coil: The Meaning of Health and Disease*. Harper & Row, 1977.

Wertenbaker, Lael Tucker. *Death of a Man*. Boston: Beacon, 1974.

Winter, Arthur, ed. *The Moment of Death: A Symposium*. Springfield, Ill.: Thomas, 1965.

Worcester, Alfred. *The Care of the Aging, the Dying, and the Dead*. 2nd ed. Springfield, Ill.: Thomas, 1961.